The Siblings'
BUSY
BOOK

Heather Kempskie
and
Lisa Hanson

 Meadowbrook Press
Distributed by Simon & Schuster
New York

Library of Congress Cataloging-in-Publication Data

Hanson, Lisa, 1973-
  The siblings' busy book : 200 fun activities for kids of different ages / by Lisa Hanson
and Heather Kempskie.
      p. cm.
  Includes index.
  ISBN-10: 0-88166-530-4, ISBN-13: 978-0-88166-530-7 (Meadowbrook Press),
  ISBN-10: 0-684-05785-9, ISBN-13: 978-0-684-05785-9 (Simon & Schuster)
  1. Amusements. 2. Games. 3. Creative activities and seat work. 4. Brothers and sisters.
I. Kempskie, Heather. II. Title.
  GV1203.H336 2008
  790.1'922--dc22

                                        2008012286

Editor: Alicia Ester
Copyeditor: Megan McGinnis
Proofreader: Angela Wiechmann
Production Manager: Paul Woods
Graphic Design Manager: Tamara Peterson
Typesetting: Danielle White
Cover Illustrations: Dorothy Stott
Cover Photo: David Young-Wolff
Interior Illustrations: Laurel Aiello

Published by Meadowbrook Press, 5451 Smetana Drive, Minnetonka, Minnesota 55343

www.meadowbrookpress.com

BOOK TRADE DISTRIBUTION by Simon and Schuster, a division of Simon and Schuster, Inc.,
1230 Avenue of the Americas, New York, New York 10020

11 10 09 08   10 9 8 7 6 5 4 3 2 1

Printed in the United States of America

Dedication

To Mom and Dad, our biggest fans—thank you for teaching us that family always comes first. To our sister Amy, our first playmate—thanks for always letting us lead you in play, even when it meant dressing you up in silly costumes for neighborhood plays.

To our husbands, Matt and Kevin, and our children Kyle, Noah, Brooke, and Jake—you are our daily inspiration.

Acknowledgments

We'd like to acknowledge the many people who joined us on this wonderful journey:

Our parents and younger sister, who planted the first seeds of the joys the sibling relationship can bring.

Our children, Kyle, Noah, Brooke, and Jake. Thank you for the wonderful moments you bring to our lives. Thank you also for helping us; we judged the quality of these activities by your reactions and smiles.

Our amazing husbands, Kevin and Matt, our team behind the scenes. These men edited, listened, gave pep talks, and brought us snacks during late-night sessions. They believed in our dreams, but more importantly, they believed in us. We love you!

Our many friends who shared their ideas, encouragement, and support. Thank you for your contributions.

And finally the wonderful team at Meadowbrook Press, who became our daily e-mail companions. Thank you to Bruce Lansky, who believed in the idea and gave us a chance; to Megan McGinnis for her positive, you-can-do-it attitude; to Alicia Ester for her coordination and seeing us to the finish line; and to Angela Wiechmann for her incredible attention to detail. This team produces and demands the highest-quality material for the parenting community. It has been an honor and privilege to learn from them.

Contents

Introduction vii

Chapter 1:
Rainy Day Fun 1

Chapter 2:
Let's Pretend 43

Chapter 3:
Music & Movement 75

Chapter 4:
Outdoor Adventures 119

Chapter 5:
Out & About 165

Chapter 6:
Learning & Exploring 183

Chapter 7:
Team Family 225

Chapter 8:
World Family 255

Chapter 9:
Arts & Crafts 275

Chapter 10:
In the Kitchen 335

Chapter 11:
Seasons & Holidays 357

Index 429

Introduction

Kids need a lot of experience having good times together so that when conflicts and fights come...they both have the memory of a positive relationship they want to get back to.

Adele Faber and Elaine Mazlish, *Siblings without Rivalry*

As twins, there's not much we haven't done together. Growing up, we spent a lot of time with each other playing, attending school, and reaching milestones. We learned early on how to exchange ideas, compromise, be creative, and share good times.

When we became adults, our bond remained strong and we continued to experience major life events together. We had our first children five months apart and gave birth to our second children *three weeks* apart. Near the end of our second pregnancies, we once ran an errand to a local department store. As we waddled through the aisles, we hardly noticed the other shoppers gawking at the very pregnant identical twins. We were intently discussing our growing families. What would it be like to have more than one child? As our children grew, would they be close? How could we make spending time together fun?

We felt we were doing a pretty decent job parenting one child each. After we had mastered the basics of feeding and clothing, we adored the time we spent reading, exploring, and playing with our sons. We wondered, could such fun be had once our sons had siblings?

We soon learned the answer to that question: *You bet it could!*

Not long after welcoming our second children to our families, we discovered that many of the activities we enjoyed with our older children could be modified so our younger ones could share the fun. We found great new ways to spend time with all our kids at the same time, using the same simple materials. Much to our pleasure, our children were having a wonderful time together. Sibling bonding was off to an excellent start!

We started sharing our ideas with friends and family members who, like us, longed for sibling activities that were easy to do, required simple materials, and encouraged positive interactions among their children. Their enthusiastic response to our suggestions prompted us to conclude that other parents and caregivers of multiple children might benefit from our ideas, too. That conclusion culminated into the book you're holding in your hands: *The Siblings' Busy Book*, the newest addition to Meadowbrook Press's popular Busy Book line.

About This Book

You'll find over two hundred activities in this book, and each has been designed to engage multiple children of varying ages. All the activities have been parent-tested and sibling-approved! We've organized the book in themed chapters so you can easily find ideas for fun play outdoors and out on the town, plus indoor activities for when the weather keeps you inside. We've also included ideas for creative movement and music, kitchen adventures, learning exploration, arts and crafts, pretend play, seasonal celebrations, and more. In addition, we offer fun and positive ways your children can work together as a family and make their world a better place.

Here's what you'll find in each activity:

- An easy-to-reference grid listing the materials you'll need for all ages plus specific age groups
- A brief overview explaining setup and general instructions
- Developmentally appropriate guidelines for four separate age groups (baby, toddler, preschooler, and school-age child)

Throughout the book, we've also included detailed illustrations, helpful parent tips, and personal anecdotes about our own experiences enjoying these activities with our children.

Regardless of your children's ages, we suggest reading each activity in its entirety before getting started. This will not only give you the complete overview of the activity, but it will also allow you to tailor the activity to your children's unique interests and abilities. Because children develop at different rates, you may find a suggestion for another age group will work better for your child. For instance, in the activity "Strollin' through Nature," your toddler may want to sort nature objects —the suggested activity for his age group—but he may also want to participate in the guessing game listed under the preschooler instructions. This is a book that can grow with your family!

We also encourage you and your children to be creative with each activity. Don't be afraid to modify them to better suit your play area, climate, or your children's moods and interests.

Let the Sibling Fun Begin!

Writing this book together reminded us how special our own sibling relationship is. We realize that sibling fun never has to end! Our hope for *The Siblings' Busy Book* is that it'll help your children learn to love and depend on one another throughout their lifetimes. Whether you have two children or ten, our wish is that this book will give you the right combination of inspiration, motivation, and ideas to help you raise children who are healthy, happy, and strongly connected to one another. If you have any questions or comments about this book, you can e-mail us or write us in care of Meadowbrook Press. We'd love to hear from you!

Heather A. Kempskie   Lisa A. Hanson

P.S. In recognition of that fact that kids do indeed come in two sexes, we alter the use of masculine and feminine pronouns throughout this book.

CHAPTER 1
Rainy Day Fun

My sons love rainy days. When it's pouring outside, we linger in our pajamas longer, enjoy breakfast at a more leisurely pace, and claim the day as ours.

—Lisa

It's easy for kids—and parents—to feel cooped up when it rains, but in this chapter, you'll find simple and fun activities to bring out the sunny side of bad weather! We've included our favorite indoor activities and games, like building with blocks and playing hide-and-seek, plus silly art projects and creative games that will get kids moving. There's even an indoor picnic. These activities may have your children wishing for rain!

Having a Rolling Ball

Here's a fun game sure to topple the rainy-day blues.

What You'll Need	All Ages	Baby	Toddler	Preschooler	School-Age Child
Empty plastic bottles (or disposable cups)	✋				
Brightly colored balls	✋				

Set up the plastic bottles to serve as bowling pins in a hallway or a large room with lots of open space. Your children can roll the balls toward the pins to knock them down.

Baby

If your baby is older than six months, you can help her roll a ball toward the pins. For an interactive activity, have one of her siblings roll a ball slowly toward her. She may even be able to grab the ball and roll it back. If your baby is younger than six months, she may have fun just watching her siblings knock down bottles with colorful balls.

Toddler

As your toddler grows, he will explore his ability to manipulate objects. You or your school-age child can show him how to bowl by spreading his legs and bending over to roll the ball "granny style" toward the bottles. Trying to knock down the bottles will challenge his hand-eye coordination—let him stand as close to the pins as he needs to!

Preschooler

As your preschooler becomes better at controlling the direction of the ball, his ability to focus will intensify. Add another challenge to this activity: After he knocks down the bottles, retrieve the ball and roll it back for him to catch.

School-Age Child

Challenge your school-age child by giving her a smaller ball to roll. She can keep track of the number of pins she knocks over, then try to beat her record each time. She can also help reset the bottles after each sibling's turn. Suggest she set them up in different formations.

Parent Tip

Your baby will be ready for sign language at about six months of age. Teach your children the sign for *ball*. Hold your arms in front of you, hands apart as if holding a ball, then slowly bring your hands toward each other.

Hide-and-Seek Sounds

Sounds will help lead your children to their siblings in this hide-and-seek game.

What You'll Need	All Ages	Baby	Toddler	Preschooler	School-Age Child
Objects that make sounds, including spoons, musical toys, blocks, or bells	✋				

Have one child (the seeker) count to ten with his or her eyes closed while your other children (the hiders) hide. You and your older children can partner up with the baby or toddler. Each hider should have an item that makes a sound. To keep the hiding area manageable, have the kids hide in only a few adjoining rooms.

Baby

Instruct your older children to make noise with their objects so your baby can locate them (with your help). During the first year, your baby is learning about object permanency, the understanding that objects exist even when unseen. Searching for the source of a sound will lead your baby to someone she loves–her sibling! Your baby can also hide and create noise (with your help).

Toddler

Like your baby, your toddler may need help when it's her turn to seek. This part of the game is a great opportunity to practice counting to ten! Slowly count with her and then say, "Ready or not, here we come!" As a hider, your toddler will discover how different objects can make different sounds. She can make loud noises with them or soft noises. While she waits for her siblings to find her, the anticipation will surely lead to giggles.

Preschooler

Your preschooler will love going solo when it's his turn to seek. He'll probably find everyone rather quickly! As a hider, he may find clever hiding spaces to keep his siblings guessing. Because it's no fun to hide in one spot too long, expect your preschooler to make plenty of noise to attract the seeker.

School-Age Child

When your school-age child is the seeker, he'll thrill his siblings if he says something like, "I can't seem to find my brother. Where *is* he?" When it's his turn to hide, give him the option to create sounds with his voice. Maybe he'll want to sound like a beating drum or a hooting owl.

Shadow, Shadow on the Wall

Introducing the family shadow show, starring your kids' adorable hands and fingers!

What You'll Need	All Ages	Baby	Toddler	Preschooler	School-Age Child
Flashlight	🖐				
Black paper					🖐
Child-safe scissors					🖐

Grab a flashlight and dim the lights. Have your children face a wall and shine the light in front of them. Let them follow the light as you make it dance across the wall and ceiling. Hold a hand in front of the light to cast a shadow on the wall and wiggle your fingers to create a spider shadow. Now it's your kids' turn to cast shadows. One of them can hold the flashlight steady as another casts a shadow.

Baby

The flashlight's bright light will transfix your baby as she develops her ability to visually track moving objects. If she is mobile, she may enjoy trying to catch the light. Point the flashlight on the floor directly in front of her and move it slowly away as she tries to catch it.

Toddler

For a fantastic cognitive exercise, let your toddler hold the flashlight. He will begin to recognize that the light moves when his hand does. When it's his turn to cast shadows, you or an older sibling can hold the flashlight for him. Encourage your toddler to wiggle his fingers to create a spider. He can make his spider fast, slow, silly, or sleepy. Describing the spider is a great way to build his growing understanding of adjectives.

Preschooler

Let your preschooler practice manipulating her fingers and hands any way she chooses. Encourage her to use her imagination to describe her shadow inventions to her siblings. For a fun guessing game, have her make animal sounds to accompany her shadow creations. Her siblings can try to guess what animals she's making. If she wants assistance, show her how to make a dog shadow: Have her press her palms together, bending her thumbs to create ears. She can move her ring and pinky fingers together to open and close the dog's mouth.

School-Age Child

With practice, your school-age child's shadows may be more sophisticated. He may even teach his siblings a few tricks! For even more fun, provide him with black paper and scissors. He can cut out small shapes in the paper, then hold it in front of the flashlight to cast more elaborate shadows. For instance, he can cut small holes to create a starry sky or he can cut out a half-moon shape to create a peaceful night scene.

Parent Tip
In addition to making shadow puppets, have your kids move their bodies closer to and farther from the flashlight, making their shadows bigger and smaller.

Hoop Ball Toss

Shoot baskets inside with this fun tossing game.

What You'll Need	All Ages	Baby	Toddler	Preschooler	School-Age Child
Hula-Hoop	🖐				
Two couch cushions (or two chairs)	🖐				
Balls	🖐				

While your children hunt for all the balls they can find, place two couch cushions on the floor and sandwich a Hula-Hoop upright between them. (You can also prop the hoop between two chairs.) Make sure there's enough space around the hoop and the cushions so your kids can get around them easily.

Baby

If your baby is crawling, encourage him to crawl through the hoop. Then kneel in front of the hoop with him and see if he can toss a small ball through it. If he's younger than six months, lay him on his back and gently roll a soft ball (a beach ball works well) over his tummy, legs, and arms. This action will help him become aware of his body parts.

Toddler

When tossing the ball, your toddler can stand as close to the hoop as he'd like. Before he makes each toss, count a hearty

"1-2-3!" to cheer him on. Station an older child on the other side of the hoop to retrieve the ball and return it to your toddler.

Preschooler

This activity is a great opportunity to teach your preschooler different ways to toss a ball. Show her how to toss it overhead, underhand, and sideways.

School-Age Child

If space allows, have your school-age child take two steps back each time she successfully tosses the ball through the hoop. She can start close to the hoop and, with skill, move back across the room. If the room is too small for this variation, see if she can toss the ball through the hoop with her eyes closed or while standing on one leg.

Jazzin' Up Junk Mail

Put your junk mail to good use with this creative and crazy activity.

What You'll Need	All Ages	Baby	Toddler	Preschooler	School-Age Child
Junk mail	🖐				
Tape	🖐				
12-inch-by-12-inch sheets of clear contact paper	🖐				
Empty tissue box			🖐		
Pencil or marker					🖐

Gather your junk mail and place it on the floor in front of your children. Announce that it's time to rip up the mail. If they don't believe you, show them by ripping up a piece! Let your children have a blast tearing and crinkling up the junk mail. They may want to tape a sheet of clear contact paper sticky side up in front of them to make fun collages with the mail pieces. (Keep your eyes open for good coupons during this activity!)

Baby

Babies love to hear crinkling and tearing paper. If your baby can sit up and is at least six months old, he can rip up some mail with his siblings. (Make sure to give him thin pieces.) Then pick out some larger pieces, put your baby in his high-chair, and tape contact paper onto the tray. With your help, let your baby stick the torn paper to the contact paper. He'll love feeling the sticky texture.

Toddler

Your toddler simply may enjoy a chance to make a mess—never mind the art project. An empty tissue box will serve as the perfect mailbox where she can stuff her junk mail scraps. Let her empty and refill the box over and over again.

Preschooler

Your preschooler will be energetic when tearing up the mail, but he may become contemplative when planning his collage. For a great motor skill activity—and a new art technique—show him how to curl a strip of torn paper by wrapping it around one of his fingers. You can also show him how to make waves or flames by making ragged tears along the edge of paper.

School-Age Child

Most pieces of junk mail are advertisements. To make his collage, your school-age child can tear out images of products he or someone in the family may like (for example, a ball for baby, a stuffed animal for toddler, a toy car for preschooler, a coffee mug for Mom). He can then label the images with his family members' names.

Crazy Sheet

Use a sheet to get your family moving and laughing together.

What You'll Need	All Ages	Baby	Toddler	Preschooler	School-Age Child
Large sheet	🖐				
Plush animal	🖐				

Spread a large sheet on the floor of a room with lots of space and have your children gather around it. Play the following games for some crazy fun!

The Wave
Have your children kneel on the floor and each hold a corner of the sheet. Tell them to wave their arms dramatically to create movement. Your baby can sit in your lap and wave his arms, too.

Popcorn
Instruct your children to hold the sheet close to the floor and quickly make little, low pops with it. If your baby can sit up, place him on the middle of the sheet. If not, lay him on the middle. He'll love watching the sheet "pop" up around him.

Parachute
Have your children hold the sheet close to the floor, then work together to raise it above their heads as quickly as possible. Then have them take a couple steps forward while lowering the sheet behind them to turn the sheet into a parachute. Let

your baby lie or sit underneath the sheet so she can watch it rise and fall around her.

Astronaut

Put an astronaut (a plush animal) on the middle of the sheet. Begin a countdown: "3-2-1, blastoff!" Raise the sheet up quickly to launch the astronaut into space. Your baby may squeal in response to the blastoff and will anticipate the next one during the countdown.

Build It Up!

Gather your budding builders and explore the fun of blocks!

What You'll Need	All Ages	Baby	Toddler	Preschooler	School-Age Child
Wood blocks in all shapes and sizes	✋				
Deck of cards					✋

Place the wood blocks on a floor or table. These simple objects will provide development stimuli for every child, regardless of age.

Baby

Small wood blocks will be fun for your baby to hold and manipulate. Show her how to knock two blocks together to make noise. If she is six months or older, she may hold one block, see a second block, then drop the first one to retrieve the second.

Toddler

Your toddler will enjoy learning how to balance, bridge, and brace the blocks to create a tower. She'll have fun knocking down the tower, too!

Preschooler

By this age, your preschooler will begin to create more recognizable objects, like skyscrapers or other buildings. If the blocks have letters on them, encourage him to build a tower that spells his name.

School-Age Child
In addition to the blocks, give your school-age child a deck of playing cards. Show him how to use two blocks to sandwich a playing card. He can do this several times and make a fence around his building. He can also make a roof for his structure by laying cards across parallel blocks. A steady table is a must!

Feather Frenzy

Get active with these fun feather games that teach patience, coordination, and teamwork.

What You'll Need	All Ages	Baby	Toddler	Preschooler	School-Age Child
Feathers (available at local craft store)	✋				
Drinking straw			✋		
Medium-size hardcover books	✋				

Feather Poem
Have each child hold a feather. As you recite the following poem, your children can act out the movements. You can assist your baby with this activity.

A feather on my hand	(Place it on hand.)
A feather tickles my cheek	(Touch it to cheek.)
A feather behind my back	(Place it behind back.)
A feather under my feet	(Brush the bottom of foot.)
A feather the tallest of all	(Hold it up in the air.)
Now watch my feather fall	(Release it.)

The poem encourages your children to bend and stretch while coordinating words with movement.

Feather Blow

Have your children lie on their bellies on the floor (an uncarpeted floor works best). Set a feather in front of each child. Encourage them to move their feathers across the floor by making an O shape with their mouths and blowing. To help your toddler direct his blowing, give him a straw to blow through. While your older children race their feathers across the floor, hold a feather in front of your baby's face and gently blow on it. You can also brush it against her cheeks and hands. She will love the soft sensation.

Feather Race

Give each child a medium-size hardcover book. Stand near your children and drop a feather. Encourage your kids to work as a team to keep the feather in the air by waving their books like fans. This is a great workout for your children's arms and a challenging hand-eye coordination activity. Your baby can't help keep the feather aloft, but she'll enjoy waving her own book or will love feeling the cool breeze from her siblings' books.

Packin' a Picnic

When it's raining outside, create some sunshine inside by enjoying an indoor family picnic.

What You'll Need	All Ages	Baby	Toddler	Preschooler	School-Age Child
Picnic snacks (see page 21)	✋				
Blanket	✋				
"Outdoor" items, such as plastic bugs, a picture of the sun, a houseplant or flowers	✋				
Paper plates, plastic utensils, and napkins	✋				
Picnic basket or paper grocery bag	✋				
Aluminum foil	✋				

Your older children can create a lovely picnic in your living room while you prepare the food. Here are some examples of picnic snacks, but feel free to create your own menu!

Baby

If your baby is six months or older, sit him in his bouncy seat for the perfect view of the picnic. He'll still be perfecting his pincher grasp, so give him some plastic spoons to play with. If he's younger than six months, lay him on the picnic blanket close to you so he can see his siblings' faces and enjoy the scents of your food.

Toddler and Preschooler

Your toddler and preschooler can spread out a blanket on the living room floor. With his older sibling's assistance, your toddler can straighten each corner. Then have them gather objects that remind them of the outdoors (for example, plastic bugs, a colored picture of the sun, a houseplant, or a vase of flowers) and place them around the blanket to create a more authentic picnic scene.

School-Age Child

Your school-age child can place plates, utensils, and napkins on the blanket as well as help you pack the picnic in a basket or grocery bag. Have her wrap the food in aluminum foil. She can play hostess by passing out the food after everyone is seated.

Parent Tip

Help set the scene for your children. Tell them to imagine that it's a beautiful, sunny day, and you're outside for a picnic. What sounds do they hear? What things do they see? This exercise can help your children for the rest of their lives. Visualization is a great tool for calming oneself in stressful situations.

Picnic Snacks

Snack	Age	Ingredients
Banana Bonanza	Baby six months or older	Mashed ripe bananas
Flower Bed	Toddler, preschooler, and school-age child	Crackers topped with hummus and sliced cucumber
Picnic Juice	Toddler, preschooler, and school-age child	Lemonade
Bug Bag	Toddler, preschooler, and school-age child	Sandwich bags filled with crackers, gummi worms, and raisins or other dried fruit (Make sure your toddler's bag has only foods approved by your pediatrician and avoid those that could pose a choking hazard.)
Ants on a Log	Preschooler and school-age child	Celery pieces topped with cream cheese (or peanut butter) and raisins

Collection Binders

Introduce your children to collecting with this simple, inexpensive activity.

What You'll Need	All Ages	Baby	Toddler	Preschooler	School-Age
Computer with printer and Internet access (or magazines)	✋				
Three-ring binders	✋				
Printer paper	✋				
Three-holed sheet protectors	✋				
Child-safe scissors	✋				
Glue sticks	✋				
Collection items					✋
Pencil					✋

This activity is a great way to discover each child's interests. Your children can collect images from your home computer or magazines for their collection binders, which they can add to again and again. If you print images from the computer, simply slip the pages into sheet protectors. When using magazine cutouts, glue them onto paper, allow them to dry, and slip them into the sheet protectors. Place each child's collection into separate binders.

Baby

For your baby's collection, ask his siblings what they think he loves. Possible items include a rattle, doll, blanket, or other small toy. Pick one item and work with your other children to find images on your computer or in magazines. Be sure to show each image to your baby while you describe it: For example, "This is a rattle." Slip the images into sheet protectors, then place them in a binder. Let your baby look through the pictures as often as possible with you and his siblings.

Toddler

Let your toddler choose a particular toy, color, or character that's most special to her. Find images of her favorite thing and let her point to the ones she wants to add to her binder. After you cut out the images, she can glue them onto the paper. With your assistance, she can then slide the paper into the sheet protectors and add the pages to her binder.

Preschooler

A collection binder gives your preschooler the opportunity to use such skills as organizing, sorting, and categorizing. Help her decide what categories are in her collection. They could include animals, people, and flowers. Write each category on a separate sheet of paper, which she can use as dividers in her binder. Have her organize her images accordingly. She can bring her collection binder with her to school, her grandparents' house, or to the park. She'll gain self-esteem by having something that reflects her unique interests.

School-Age Child
Perhaps your school-age child collects baseball cards, stickers, or toy cars. Invite him to set up a display of these items for his siblings to visit. He can write descriptions or include photos or images of his collection in his collector's binder, creating an inventory of his items.

Parent Tip
The Internet can be a wonderful resource when used properly. Take time to review Internet safety with your children and always supervise while they use the computer.

It's a Wrap

In this activity, your children will discover it's just as fun to wrap objects as it is to unwrap them.

What You'll Need	All Ages	Baby	Toddler	Preschooler	School-Age Child
Gift-wrap	🖐				
Boxes of various sizes			🖐	🖐	🖐
Objects to wrap (books, small toys, and so on)			🖐	🖐	🖐
Toy blocks		🖐			
Child-safe scissors			🖐	🖐	🖐
Tape			🖐	🖐	🖐
Stickers			🖐		
Crayons			🖐		

Break out gift-wrap and different-size boxes, and let your children wrap up objects for fun. When they're done, have them exchange "gifts" and enjoy undoing their handiwork.

Baby

If your baby is older than six months, lay some gift-wrap over a few toy blocks for her to "unwrap." Whether she's sitting in her highchair or crawling toward the hidden blocks on the floor, this hide-and-seek game will have her using her motor skills to grab and hold the paper. If your baby is younger than six months, hold a piece of brightly colored gift-wrap in front of her and slowly begin to crumple it. Hide it behind your back and crumple it again. Playfully ask your baby, "Where did that noise come from?"

Toddler
Give your toddler an empty box and invite her to place an object, like a book or small toy, in it as a pretend gift. Because wrapping the gift may be difficult for her, cut shapes from the gift-wrap and help her tape them to the box. Also provide her with some stickers and crayons to decorate her box.

Preschooler
Help your preschooler measure and cut the appropriate amount of gift-wrap. Show him how to fold the paper to cover the box, and stick pieces of tape to the edge of the table so he can easily retrieve them. Grabbing and placing the tape is an excellent motor skill exercise.

School-Age Child
Cutting gift-wrap and wrapping gifts are great ways for your school-age child to learn how to estimate, measure, and solve problems. Have him secretly wrap a object and then provide clues for his siblings as they try to guess what it is.

The Home Highway

Rev up your engines—it's time for an indoor highway game that will get your kids moving!

What You'll Need	All Ages	Baby	Toddler	Preschooler	School-Age Child
Child-safe scissors	🖐				
Red, yellow, green, and white construction paper	🖐				
Markers	🖐				
Tape	🖐				
Stroller		🖐			
Toy car			🖐		

To begin, you and your older children can create traffic signs for the family's home highway. You can include traffic lights (green, red, and yellow), stop signs, railroad-crossing signs, one-way signs, and signs with arrows pointing left, right, or straight. The kids can cut out the signs' shapes from the appropriate colors of construction paper (for example, an octagon from red paper) and add words and features with markers (for example, the word *STOP*). They can then tape the signs at eye level around your home to transform it into an active and busy street. Once the highway is complete, it's time for the whole family to go for a "drive"!

Baby

Bring your baby for a ride on the home highway. Transport her in her stroller or hold her in your arms as you zoom around. Make car noises as you travel, including screeching brakes. No matter your baby's age, she will love moving quickly and hearing your enthusiastic sounds!

Toddler

Your toddler can bring a toy car along with him or he can be the car. Point out the signs and teach him what they mean. For instance, "This big red sign says 'Stop.'" Say the word as you show him the action. He may enjoy following the signs or making up his own rules.

Preschooler and School-Age Child

Your preschooler and school-age child can help their siblings abide by the rules by serving as friendly traffic cops. Show them how to signal *stop* (palm out, fingers upward), *go* (palm inward and motioning forward), and *turn left* or *turn right* (point in the correct direction).

Parent Tip

This activity is a great opportunity to review street-crossing safety. Stand with your children on one side of the home highway and tell them to look both ways for cars. If they don't see any, it is safe to cross the street while holding a grownup's hand.

Indoor Scavenger Hunt

Your children will need determination and sleuthing skills for this indoor scavenger hunt!

What You'll Need	All Ages	Baby	Toddler	Preschooler	School-Age Child
Index cards	✋				
Markers	✋				

For each child, use markers to create three age-appropriate visual clues (drawings of objects in the home) or verbal clues (words about objects in the home) on index cards. Give the clue cards to the children, and let the scavenger hunt begin!

Baby

Give the baby's clue cards to your older children, and have them find the items for her. Your baby can enjoy the hunt, too, by crawling after her siblings or riding in your arms. After each item is found, show her the image on its index card and then show her the corresponding object.

Toddler

Give your toddler one card at a time, and give him additional hints about the objects' locations. Use prepositions to describe the items' locations, like *in, under, above, between,* and *below,* such as "This object is under the coffee table."

Preschooler

You can give your preschooler clue cards with drawings, but you may decide to give her verbal clues only, such as, "Find something you can build with that is square." This requires her to use creativity and deduction. She may find a block, a box, or anything else that fits the description.

School-Age Child

Your school-age child will be up for more of a challenge, so send him off to find several objects for each clue. His clue cards should provide challenges such as, "Find three things in the house that hold things together." He may return with some tape, a bottle of glue, and a piece of string. Another example could include, "Find three things that are each spelled with two vowels." He may return with a book, banana, and shoe.

Parent Tip

After the hunt is done, create another game to put the items away. For each item, challenge your children to return it to its proper place by the time you (or an older child) count to ten.

Where Is the Boat?

There's essentially no setup and tons of guessing fun in this game!

What You'll Need	All Ages	Baby	Toddler	Preschooler	School-Age Child
Toy boat	🖐				

Each child takes a turn being the "sailor," who stands with eyes closed facing away from the others. Hand a toy boat to one of the players and tell the child to quietly hide it. (The hiding place will depend on the sailor's age—see below. You may need to help the hider find an appropriate place for each sailor.) When it's hidden, the sailor opens his or her eyes and everyone chants:

Ahoy, [name of sailor]!
Your boat is lost at sea.
Wherever could it be!

The sailor then searches for the boat. If the sailor finds it, whoever hid the boat becomes the sailor. If the sailor doesn't find the boat, he or she remains the sailor for another turn.

Baby

When it is your baby's turn to be the sailor, have one of your children hide the boat behind his or her back while you face the other direction with your baby. After it's hidden, hold her in front of each player for a few seconds as she contemplates which sibling has the boat. She'll love looking at her playmates' expressive faces. When she reaches the hider, have the sibling dramatically reveal the boat and say "Peekaboo!"

Toddler

When it's your toddler's turn as sailor, make sure your other children know they must hide the boat somewhere in plain or partial view. Your toddler will love this game's suspense and will enjoy searching for the boat's location.

Preschooler

Encourage the hider to place the boat somewhere out of sight when it's your preschooler's turn as sailor. To make it more fun, play "hot and cold" while he is searching. Say "cold" when he's far from the toy and "hot" when he gets closer to finding it.

School-Age Child

When it's your school-age child's turn, hide the boat completely out of sight. To challenge him, give him a time limit, such as ten seconds, to find the boat.

Sharing a Smile

Just try to keep a serious face during this happy circle game!

What You'll Need	All Ages	Baby	Toddler	Preschooler	School-Age Child
Smiles!	✋				

Have your children sit in a circle. Your oldest child can start the game by smiling widely or making a funny face. His siblings must try their hardest not to smile in response. He can then use his hand to "wipe" the smile off his face, then "toss" it to one of his siblings, who then takes a turn smiling. The round ends after everyone has had a turn tossing a smile… or once everyone has started giggling. How long can your children keep the round going?

Baby
Babies love faces, and your baby will have a great view of her siblings' faces during this game. If a sibling tosses her a smile, see if you can make a grin appear on her face with a silly movement or sound.

Toddler
Most toddlers mimic the emotions of others. If your toddler sees smiling faces all around him, he may join in. Have fun showing him how to wipe a smile off his face and how to throw it. If he smiles throughout the whole game, let him and enjoy it!

Preschooler and School-Age Child

Your preschooler and school-age child are more able to control their facial expressions, so they may be champions at this game. Instead of tossing a smile, your older child may pretend to hide it under her shirt, sit on it, or pull it through her ears in an attempt to make her siblings laugh!

Puzzle Making

Take out some puzzles or create your own on a rainy afternoon!

What You'll Need	All Ages	Baby	Toddler	Preschooler	School-Age Child
Plastic balls and wooden blocks		🖐			
Shoebox with lid		🖐			
Pencil		🖐			
Scissors		🖐	🖐		
Puzzle with large pieces		🖐	🖐		
Empty cereal boxes			🖐	🖐	🖐
Crayons				🖐	🖐
Child-safe scissors				🖐	🖐

Baby

If your baby is six months or older, he can work on a home-made puzzle that's perfect for his age: a shape sorter. Gather some wooden blocks and plastic balls. On a shoebox lid, trace circles and squares big enough for the balls and blocks to fit through, then cut out the shapes. Place the lid back on the shoebox and encourage your baby to slip the balls and blocks through the circles and squares. When he's dropped all the objects into the box, empty it out so he can repeat the fun!

If your baby is younger, help him explore the odd shapes of puzzle pieces. Run his fingers along the contours of a large, chunky puzzle piece—down the curves and over the bumps.

Toddler

Place some puzzles with large, chunky pieces on the floor for your toddler to put together. You can also create a homemade puzzle: Cut the front of a cereal box into large pieces. Your toddler can work to reassemble the familiar image.

Preschooler and School-Age Child

Cut the front and back of a cereal box and give one piece to your preschooler and one to your school-age child. Have them decorate the back of the cardboard with crayons. Suggest they draw large, realistic pictures of people, vehicles, or houses. They can cut the cardboard into large, chunky pieces. Then they can mix up the pieces and try to put their puzzles back together again.

Terrific Tunnels

Turn any room into a twisty roadway complete with tunnels!

What You'll Need	All Ages	Baby	Toddler	Preschooler	School-Age Child
Large paper bags	🖐				
Scissors	🖐				
Masking tape	🖐				
Toy trucks and cars			🖐	🖐	🖐
Crayons				🖐	
Books					🖐
Blankets					🖐
Chairs					🖐

Cut out the bottoms of several paper bags. Tape the bottomless bags together end to end to create a tunnel. For wider tunnels, cut each bag along a crease, then tape two bags together where you cut. Tape your double-wide bags end to end to complete the tunnel.

Baby

Is your baby on the move and ready to explore? Cruising in the tunnels will be a new experience for him. If he is younger than six months or not crawling yet, lay him on his tummy to look through a short tunnel. Have his siblings look through the other end and play peekaboo with him.

Toddler

Your toddler may get right to work crawling through the tunnels! Taking a toy truck with her will make the journey even more exciting. This pretend play is how your toddler begins to make sense out of things she sees, like roads and cars.

Preschooler

To get through the small tunnels, your preschooler may have to army crawl (pull himself forward with his arms while dragging his legs behind him), which is great for building muscles and coordination in the upper half of his body. On his way through, he may stop to create roadways with crayons for his toy cars for subsequent trips through the tunnels.

School-Age Child

Your school-age child can create cool ramps for toy cars by propping up one end of a tunnel with some books. She can place two toy cars at the top of the tunnel and see which car goes the farthest or the quickest. She can also use blankets draped over chairs to make tunnels of her own to crawl through. Or she may find it to be a quiet place for her to read a book alone or with her siblings.

Designer Dress Up

Let your kids be fashion designers!

What You'll Need	All Ages	Baby	Toddler	Preschooler	School-Age Child
Child-safe scissors			✋	✋	✋
Cardstock			✋	✋	✋
Crayons			✋	✋	✋
Glue sticks			✋	✋	✋
Construction paper			✋	✋	✋
Plush animal		✋			
Baby clothes		✋			

Cut small shirts, pants, skirts, hats, and shoes out of cardstock. After you've cut a few pieces, encourage your children to be fashion designers and color the clothes while you continue to cut more. You may also want your preschooler and school-age child to use your cutouts as patterns to cut clothes of their own. When all the clothing is cut out and colored, have your children assemble entire outfits and glue them to construction paper. If they want, they can complete their pictures by filling in bodies and heads.

Baby

While your older children work on their projects, this is the perfect opportunity to teach your baby about clothing. Does she have a favorite plush animal? Sit close to her and let her watch you dress her favorite friend using baby clothes (a onesie, socks, or shirt). Be sure to name each item you put on her friend.

Toddler

Give your toddler a few clothing cutouts and draw a person on her construction paper. To get her started, say, "This person needs shoes. Can you find a shoe for him?" Let her gaze over her choices and applaud her efforts when she points to a shoe. Let her show you where to glue it on the figure.

Preschooler

Your preschooler will enjoy "designing" colorful garb for a trip to the beach or a fancy party. At this age, she knows where each item should go when it's time to glue her outfit to construction paper. Her sense of humor may get the best of her, though: The shoes could end up coming out of shirt sleeves!

School-Age Child

After gluing his outfit onto construction paper, encourage your school-age child to finish the scene by drawing a body and a backdrop. Ask him where his person might go in that outfit. For example, if he chose blue jeans and a T-shirt, he might draw a classroom or park in the background.

At the Movies

Rainy weather is the perfect excuse to cuddle with your family and enjoy a short movie.

What You'll Need	All Ages	Baby	Toddler	Preschooler	School-Age Child
Age- appropriate movie	✋				
Pillows and blankets	✋				
Snacks			✋	✋	✋
Construction paper and crayons			✋	✋	✋

Make watching a movie a special event by putting soft pillows and blankets on the floor, darkening the room, and cuddling together. See the "In The Kitchen" chapter for some movie-time treats.

Baby
The American Academy of Pediatrics recommends no TV for children under the age of two, so use your discretion if including your baby in this activity. We suggest you use this time to feed him or cuddle him while he rests.

Toddler, Preschooler, and School-Age Child
Make up some fun rules for your viewing time. For instance, whenever a song begins, everyone has to get up and dance.

Or if there's a bird in the movie, everyone has to pretend to fly. When the movie is done, try these fun activities:

- Discuss your favorite scenes and characters.
- Pass out construction paper and crayons, and ask your children to each draw their favorite scene.
- Re-create a scene by narrating it and having your children act it out. You may have future actors in your house!

Parent Tip
Preview a family-friendly movie or get a recommendation by visiting an online source like Yahoo!'s Movie Mom (http://movies.yahoo.com/mv/moviemom/).

CHAPTER 2
Let's Pretend

A dear friend of mine once told me about her five-year-old daughter's pretend play with future careers. The little girl had pretended to be a marine biologist—who was also a Mary Kay lady. She just had one question: "Can I have a day off?"

"Of course," her mom replied. "Most people have weekends off."

"Good," she said as she skipped out of the room. "That means I'll be a mermaid on weekends!"

—Heather

Is there anything as strong as a child's imagination? All children love pretend play, and they usually find it most enjoyable when others join them, which makes it the perfect pastime for sibling fun. In this chapter, we offer imagination-boosting activities that use simple props from around the home. With special instructions to stimulate each age range, your kids will become astronauts, hairstylists, and doctors right before your eyes!

Check-Us-Out Library

Nurture your children's love of reading by setting up a library in your home.

What You'll Need	All Ages	Baby	Toddler	Preschooler	School-Age Child
Books	✋				
Index cards or slips of paper	✋				
Post-it Notes			✋		
Stamp and ink pad				✋	

Have your children gather a variety of books to create their library. They can display the books on tables, chairs, shelves, or the floor. Set up a checkout station and give each patron an index card or slip of paper as a library card.

Baby

Your baby can be the first patron of this special library. Select a brightly illustrated board book for her to handle and mouth. Read the story to her or invite an older child to read it to everyone. Your baby will associate reading as a special time with you and her siblings.

Toddler

Your toddler can help place a Post-it Note checkout card inside the front cover of every book, but he'll enjoy being a library patron more. He likely has a few favorite books that he recognizes by their covers, so don't be surprised if he selects them when it's his turn to check out books.

Preschooler

Let your preschooler play the librarian. Set him up at the checkout station. He can use a stamp and ink pad to mark "due dates" on the checkout cards. He can also help patrons select books. Say to him, "I feel like reading a funny book. Can you select one for me, Mr. Librarian?"

School-Age Child

Your school-age child can decide how to display and organize the books in the family library. For example, does she want to group the books by age range? Topic? Alphabetical author or title? When she's done, have her give the patrons a tour of the library.

Mail for You and Me

Send and deliver mail right in your own home!

What You'll Need	All Ages	Baby	Toddler	Preschooler	School-Age Child
Paper grocery bag	🖐				
Child-safe scissors	🖐				
Stapler	🖐				
Crayons			🖐		
Index cards			🖐	🖐	🖐
Large purse or lunch bag			🖐		
Envelopes				🖐	🖐
Stickers				🖐	
Pencil					🖐

To create a mailbox, close the top of a paper grocery bag, then fold it over and staple it shut. Cut a 6-inch-by-2-inch slot in the front of the bag. Your children can then get busy writing, sending, and delivering their letters.

Baby
Sing this twist on Woody Guthrie's "Mail Myself to You" with your older kids while taking turns doing the following actions with your baby:

I am going to fold you up like an envelope. (Fold his arms gently with your hands.)

Put glue on your nose—you will see. (Gently tap his nose.)
Put stamps upon your head. (Gently tap his head.)
And mail you straight to me! (Hug him.)

Toddler

Draw different shapes with a crayon on separate index cards
and give them to your toddler. She can deliver these pretend
postcards. For example, ask her to deliver the card with a circle
to the baby or place the card with the square in the mailbox.
She can even use her own mailbag (a purse or lunch bag) to
make her deliveries.

Preschooler

Give your preschooler the supplies needed to send letters. He can
stuff index cards into envelopes, put "stamps" (stickers) on the
envelopes, and put the envelopes into the mailbox. Later, he can
pretend to be a letter carrier and deliver the mail to his siblings.

School-Age Child

Let your school-age child gather the
mail from the mailbox and prepare it
for delivery. She can decide where
each letter should be mailed by
writing the name and
address of a family
member on each
envelope.

Toy Store Sale

Make the toys in your home seem brand-new by setting up a pretend toy store.

What You'll Need	All Ages	Baby	Toddler	Preschooler	School-Age Child
Toys	✋				
Play money	✋				
Paper grocery bags			✋		
Post-it Notes				✋	
Crayons				✋	
Shoebox or muffin pan					✋

Have your children each find a few toys to "sell," then help them create a toy store in a room in your home. Give each child some play money, and let them choose the toys they wish to buy!

Baby

Assign a sibling to select a few items just right for your baby and demonstrate to him how they work. For instance, a child may race a toy car in front of the baby. He will love the inter-action and may try to imitate his sibling at play. He will also love to hold, examine, and play with the toys picked especially for him.

Toddler

Your toddler loves to load and unload objects, making her the perfect person to stock the toy store! She can place toys on tables or couches and help load paper bags with merchandise. To sharpen her listening skills and build her language skills, pretend to be a shopper and ask for "big" or "noisy" toys. She will try to identify the toys that meet your requests.

Preschooler

Give your preschooler Post-it Notes to place on each toy. On them, she can write how much each toy costs. Have her use denominations that match the play money. Help her decide the cost of each toy based on its size and how fancy it is. This activity is a wonderful way to practice number recognition and introduce the value of money.

School-Age Child

This activity is perfect for strengthening your school-age child's math skills. He can use a shoebox or muffin pan as a cash register, then collect the money and make change when someone makes a purchase.

Camping In

You don't have to be outdoors to enjoy this campsite!

What You'll Need	All Ages	Baby	Toddler	Preschooler	School-Age Child
Metal pots and pans	🖐				
Wooden spoon	🖐				
Bell		🖐			
Toy blocks	🖐				
Red and yellow tissue paper	🖐				
Blankets and pillows	🖐				
Large sheet (or chairs and rope or a real tent)	🖐				

Setting up camp is a big part of the fun. Your children can help with the setup before enjoying the camping activities listed on the next page.

Baby

As your baby's siblings set up camp, she can keep "wild animals" at bay. If she's old enough to sit up by herself, give her a metal pot and a wooden spoon and let her bang away. Or give her a bell to jingle. If she is younger, jingle the bell in front of her. She'll enjoy the tinkling sound.

Toddler

With help, your toddler can create a pretend campfire. She can arrange toy blocks in a circle and place crumpled red and yellow tissue paper in the center of the circle.

Preschooler

Your preschooler can do a number of tasks around camp. He can gather pots and pans for a pretend cookout. Once the tent is pitched, he can arrange the blankets and pillows inside it.

School-Age Child

To create a tent, your school-age child can drape a large sheet over a table or set up two chairs, tie a rope between them, and drape a blanket over the rope. Or, if possible, you can help him set up a real tent.

Parent Tip

Here are some creative ways to enjoy the campsite together:

- Read stories around the campfire.
- Prepare a pretend meal of hot dogs and baked beans.
- Hike the area around your campsite.
- Fish in a make-believe lake (a blue blanket or sheet spread on the floor).
- Search for wildlife. Hide a few plush animals under chairs or tables and have your children search for them.

Barnyard Fun

Your little farmers will love creating their own barn for their plush and plastic animals.

What You'll Need	All Ages	Baby	Toddler	Preschooler	School-Age Child
Blanket	🖐				
Plush and plastic farm animals	🖐				
Indoor riding toy			🖐		
Buckets or plastic bowls			🖐		
Brush			🖐		
Hobbyhorse or large stick				🖐	🖐

Use a blanket draped over chairs to create an indoor barn. Let your children complete the scene with plush or plastic farm animals.

Baby

Babies often learn and repeat one-syllable words before learning more complicated ones. This activity may encourage your baby to make an animal sound, perhaps as a first word! Sit in front of your baby and repeat an animal sound like "moo" or "oink" while slowly exaggerating your lip movements. See if he will repeat the sound. To help your baby associate objects and sounds, hold up a plush animal while making the appropriate sound.

Toddler

If your toddler has an indoor riding toy, have him use it as a tractor around the barnyard. He can deliver toy buckets or plastic bowls filled with imaginary hay or feed for the animals. Encourage him to groom the animals by giving him a small brush to use.

Preschooler and School-Age Child

Give your preschooler and school-age child some riding lessons with a hobbyhorse (or a large stick). Show them how to straddle the horse and ride around the barn. To challenge their motor skills, have them walk, trot, and gallop the horse.

Uppity-Do Hairdressers

Take turns creating fun, goofy, or slick new dos at your family salon.

What You'll Need	All Ages	Baby	Toddler	Preschooler	School-Age Child
Pillow	✋				
Hats	✋				
Spray bottle with water	✋				
Baby brush		✋			
Hand mirror	✋				
Wide-tooth comb	✋				
Hair accessories, such as ribbons, clips, elastic ponytail holders	✋				
Hair gel					✋

Your children can take turns styling one another's hair. Depending on the height of the stylist, have the customer sit on a pillow (for comfort) on a chair or the floor so the stylist can easily reach the hair. Put the styling supplies on a nearby table.

Baby

Because your baby's scalp and skull are fragile, it's best not to let your other children style her hair. Instead, they can place a large hat on her head and gently take it off for a fun peekaboo game. Or you can be the stylist for her. Your baby doesn't need a full head of hair to be a great customer! Mist her head with water and use a baby brush to gently brush her scalp or hair. Hold a mirror in front of her face so she can admire her do.

Toddler
Your toddler can hold a hand mirror and watch his sibling style his hair. He may especially enjoy accessories like hats or clips. When it's his turn to be the stylist, let him use a wide-tooth comb. Remind him to be gentle! Combing hair is a good exercise for his hand muscles.

Preschooler
Preschoolers love to imitate others. If your preschooler has watched you style his siblings' hair, he'll likely repeat some of your actions. Let him use a spray bottle to wet his customer's hair, then comb it out and add accessories to it.

School-Age Child
Your school-age child may want to try some advanced styling techniques on her customers' hair. Show her how to braid the hair or pull it into a ponytail. She may also choose to use hair gel to sculpt spikes or waves.

Checkup at the Doctor's Office

Your kids will love being doctors and fixing boo-boos!

What You'll Need	All Ages	Baby	Toddler	Preschooler	School-Age Child
Books, magazines, and toys	🖐				
Blanket and pillow	🖐				
Doctor's kit items, such as thermometer (straw), stethoscope (head-phones), prescription pad (note pad)	🖐				
White adult-size T-shirt	🖐				
Large sheet of paper, crayons, and tape				🖐	

You and your children can set up the play area like a doctor's office. Create a waiting room by setting out chairs, books and magazines, and toys. Make an examination room in another part of the area by setting out a couple of chairs and laying a blanket and pillow on the floor. Gather items to make a doctor's kit, then let your kids take turns playing the doctor and the patient. The doctor can put on a large white T-shirt, then pretend to check the patient's temperature with a "thermometer," listen to her heart with a "stethoscope," put a Band-Aid on a cut, and even write out a prescription!

Baby
Your baby will make a great patient. Have her doctors count her toes, look into her eyes, and make her smile. She will love the interaction and will begin to bond with her siblings.

Toddler
When your toddler is the doctor, make requests such as, "Will you please check my ears? Where are my ears? How many ears do I have?" This is a fun way to teach her about anatomy. To keep her attention while she is the patient, keep the "exam" action-packed!

Preschooler
Your preschooler can design a vision test for his patients. Have him write a few letters on a large sheet of paper. Tape the paper to a wall, then the patients can take turns reading the letters out loud. For a more realistic vision test, the patient can block one eye with a hand while identifying the letters.

School-Age Child
Your school-age child can have fun writing prescriptions for his patients' pretend ills. For example, he can write, "Eat two cookies." Encourage him to sign his name with a flourish on the prescription.

Animal Hospital

Give some beloved plush animals a dose of TLC at this family-operated animal hospital.

What You'll Need	All Ages	Baby	Toddler	Preschooler	School-Age Child
Plush animals	✋				
Blankets	✋				
Vet kit items, such as a stethoscope (head-phones), otoscope (spoon), brush, and Band-Aids				✋	✋
Stickers			✋		
Shoebox				✋	✋

While your children round up some plush animals, designate an area to be the waiting room with some chairs. To create the examination room, lay a small blanket on the floor and place the vet kit nearby. Your older children can take turns playing the veterinarian and the pet owner while your younger children play the animal hospital staff.

Baby

Your baby can be the waiting room attendant. Let her sit on the floor among the plush animals. She may enjoy reaching for them, touching their soft fur, and gazing at their faces.

Hold one close to her and make the animal's sounds. She'll enjoy listening to the noises.

Toddler

Your toddler may enjoy being the vet assistant in charge of bringing the patients in and out of the examination room. Show him how to wrap each animal in a blanket. He can even place stickers on the animals for being brave during the examination!

Preschooler and School-Age Child

Your preschooler and school-age child can take turns being the veterinarian and the pet owner. The vet can ask, "What happened to your pet? Has he eaten lately?" then examine the animal using the vet kit. He can provide a diagnosis such as, "He needs a Band-Aid and rest!" The pet owner can ask questions such as, "How can I help my pet feel better?" Let her bring her pet home using a carrier fashioned from a shoebox. Simply remove the shoebox lid and place the animal inside.

Planes, Trains, and Automobiles

With some imagination, your children can really go places!

What You'll Need	All Ages	Baby	Toddler	Preschooler	School-Age Child
Large towels	✋				
Couch cushions or pillows	✋				
Fan	✋				
Tissues	✋				
Old keys				✋	
Plastic plate					✋

Below you'll find four transportation games you can play as a family even though they are each geared toward specific age groups. After setting up each game, let your children use their imaginations to create the experience: Where are they going? What do they see? What happens during the ride?

Baby

Your baby will love playing "Train." Roll two large towels per child lengthwise and lay them on the floor parallel to each other and about two feet apart. Have your children sit between the towels. Encourage them to bounce up and down as they make train noises like, "*Chugga, chugga, choo, choo!*" Your baby can either sit in your arms or sit propped against rolled-up towels. Or he can get some tummy time by lying over a rolled-up towel.

Toddler

Your toddler will enjoy "Plane." Place soft pillows or cushions in a line, one behind another, and have your children sit on them. To feel as though you're soaring through the clouds, turn on a small fan in front of the first pillow. (Be sure the fan is out of reach of small hands.) Then encourage your kids to hold out their arms like wings. Your toddler may enjoy being the pilot on the first cushion. He can release tissues into the breeze from the fan. To his passengers, the tissues will look like passing clouds!

Preschooler

"Car" is geared for your preschooler! Set out pillows in two rows. They'll become seats for your car. Have your preschooler sit in the driver's seat and encourage your other kids to climb in, too. If you like, give your preschooler real car keys to start her car. Have her act out putting on a seat belt, checking mirrors, beeping the horn, stopping at red lights, and so on.

School-Age Child

"Bus" is the perfect game for your school-age child. Set out chairs or lay pillows on the floor to create rows of seats. Set a chair in front of the first row. Let your school-age child be the bus driver. Give her a plastic plate as a steering wheel, and have her open the bus door to let her siblings on board. If she rides a bus to school, encourage her to teach her siblings the rules of safe bus riding. If you like, sing "The Wheels on the Bus" with your kids as your school-age child drives from stop to stop.

Walk on the Moon

Turn your living room into the surface of the moon and let your kids explore!

What You'll Need	All Ages	Baby	Toddler	Preschooler	School-Age Child
Child-safe scissors	🖐				
Paper bags	🖐				
Stickers and crayons	🖐				
String			🖐	🖐	🖐
Large and small sponges			🖐	🖐	🖐
Blankets and pillows	🖐				

Before you launch your astronauts into outer space, equip them properly: Create a space helmet for each child by cutting out a large square from the front of a paper bag. If your kids like, they can decorate their helmets as well as the baby's helmet with stickers and crayons, then they can place them over their heads. For moon shoes, use string to attach large sponges, like the kind used to wash a car, to the bottoms of your preschooler's and school-age child's feet. Use kitchen sponges for your toddler.

To create a rocket, set out four chairs to be the corners of a 5-foot-by-5-foot square. Drape a blanket over the chairs. Invite your children to lie on their backs inside the rocket, much as real astronauts are positioned during takeoff. Finally, create a

moon surface while the kids wait to blast off by laying pillows
and crumpled blankets on the floor as craters and rocks.

Baby

Lay your baby on her back on a blanket for a fun blastoff game.
Give a countdown: "10, 9, 8, 7, 6, 5, 4, 3, 2, 1..." Then shout
"BLASTOFF!" and raise her to the sky. She'll love the anticipa-
tion and the motion!

Toddler

When the rocket lands on the moon, encourage your toddler
to navigate the surface. Walking in his moon shoes around the
craters and rocks will take concentration and will be good
exercise for him!

Preschooler and School-Age Child

What adventures will your preschooler and school-age child
have on the moon? Encourage them to go on moonwalks, collect samples from the surface, take images of the moonscape,
and repair space equipment. While playing, tell them the
names of the planets on our solar system (Mercury, Venus,
Earth, Mars, Jupiter, Saturn, Uranus, Neptune) and discuss
what else astronauts do in space.

If the Shoe Fits

Your kids will love trying on different styles and sizes of shoes in their own shoe store.

What You'll Need	All Ages	Baby	Toddler	Preschooler	School-Age Child
Various shoes	✋				
Shoeboxes				✋	
Tape measure or ruler					✋

Have your children gather as many pairs of shoes as they like. Help them arrange the pairs in a designated area that will become their shoe store. Let them have fun trying on different pairs of shoes in different sizes.

Baby

Pick out shoes with textured soles, like a smooth dress shoe, a rubbery sneaker, and a rough work boot. Gently rub each sole on your baby's foot to stimulate the thousands of nerve endings. She'll love the different sensations!

Toddler

Toddlers are still mastering walking. If your toddler can walk skillfully, have him try on a few pairs of shoes to test his balance. He may want to slip on a pair of your shoes or an older sibling's. For some pretend play, call him by the shoe owner's name. You can also pretend to be a customer sending him on a search for a specific pair of shoes, like blue shoes or shiny ones.

Preschooler

Let your preschooler organize the shoe store by matching up the pairs of shoes and displaying them in any order she wants. Perhaps she'll arrange the pairs by size or by color. She may also enjoy using shoeboxes to package sales. If your preschooler has trouble knowing which shoe goes on which foot, this activity is a great time to reinforce the idea. Point out how one side of every shoe curves inward. Then encourage her to place a pair of shoes together, facing forward with the curves touching, in front of her feet. The left shoe will be in front of her left foot, and the right shoe will be in front of her right foot.

School-Age Child

Let your school-age child measure everyone's feet with a tape measure or ruler. He can lay the tool on the floor and ask each person to stand next to it while he records the length. Who has the smallest feet? The largest? If he adds the measurements together, what number does he get?

Cool School Days

Let the learning begin in a pretend school in your home!

What You'll Need	All Ages	Baby	Toddler	Preschooler	School-Age Child
Coloring books, paper, crayons, and books	🖐				
Chalkboard (or black construction paper and tape)	🖐				
Book bag			🖐		
Chalk				🖐	
Ruler				🖐	

Create a space in your home to serve as a classroom. Set up a few work stations that include coloring books, paper, crayons, and books. You can even set up a small chalkboard, if you have one. (Or you can create a "chalkboard" by taping black construction paper to the wall.) Your children will have fun teaching one another art, reading, and writing!

Baby

Babies may make the perfect students: they are both observant and curious. Your baby's "teachers" can entice her senses by sharing colorful pages from a book or by singing songs to her.

67

Toddler

When it's your toddler's turn to be the teacher, help her get into character by giving her a bag to carry some books. She may want to pass out paper and crayons to her students. What does she want them to draw? Encourage her to call out ideas like "bird" or "tree."

Preschooler

A great way for your preschooler to practice writing and identifying letters is for him to teach them to his siblings. Have him write his name on the chalkboard. Give him a ruler to point to each letter as he recites them to his students. Take this time to teach him how to spell simple words like *cat* and *dog*, then let him point out each letter to the students.

School-Age Child

Your school-age child can take attendance when he is the teacher. Have him call each sibling's name. His students can respond, "Here!" To practice reading out loud, he can read a story to his students. Encourage him to ask them about the book. Who was in it? How did it end? Were there any silly parts in the story?

When I was a child, my favorite thing to play was school. I used to prop up my baby sister on pillows and surround her with books and other students (my plush animals). I would read to her and show her pictures!

—Lisa

Dining Out

Let your children open their own restaurant complete with play food and a menu.

What You'll Need	All Ages	Baby	Toddler	Preschooler	School-Age Child
Magazines	🖐				
Child-safe scissors	🖐				
Construction paper	🖐				
Crayons	🖐				
Glue sticks	🖐				
Paper plates and napkins	🖐				
Place mats	🖐				
Plastic play food	🖐				
Notepad and pencil				🖐	
Apron					🖐
Pots, pans, and cooking utensils					🖐

Designate a space in your home to serve as the family restaurant. Your children can search through magazines to find images of food to cut out for the menu. To make the menu, help your children fold a sheet of construction paper lengthwise and widthwise to make four sections. Your or your school-age child can label the sections "Drinks," "Dinners," "Side Dishes," and "Desserts." Have your children glue the food images onto the appropriate section. Finally, encourage your kids to set the table with paper plates and napkins. If you like, use the place mats from "Trace a Place Mat" (see page 278).

Baby

Your baby can patronize the restaurant. Set her in her high-chair or bouncy seat and let her siblings show her the menu. With a small gurgle or movement, she can indicate her choice, or the server can surprise her! Have the server bring her play food she can explore.

Toddler

Your toddler can take turns being a server and a patron. Challenge her to balance play food on plates when serving her customers. No worries if she spills! When she's a restaurant patron, your toddler will enjoy making her own decisions by pointing to her order on the menu. Encourage her to order an item from each section.

Preschooler

Your preschooler will enjoy being a patron, but he may prefer working on the restaurant floor. Let him greet and seat guests and take orders by jotting marks on a notepad. He can also bus the tables. Maybe he'll get a tip!

School-Age Child

Your school-age child can staff the kitchen and serve as the restaurant chef. Let him wear an apron and use some pots and pans as he pretends to prepare scrumptious foods in a designated "kitchen" area. A small table can serve as a counter, sink, or stove. He may also enjoy leaving the cooking to someone else as he takes turns as a patron.

Let's Go Grocery Shopping

Open your kitchen cabinets and let your children set up a grocery store.

What You'll Need	All Ages	Baby	Toddler	Preschooler	School-Age Child
Canned and boxed food items	✋				
Play money	✋				
Paper bags	✋				
Stroller		✋			
Post-it note and pencil				✋	
Poster board					✋
Crayons or magazines, child-safe scissors, and glue					✋

Encourage your children to find canned and boxed food in your kitchen cupboards. (Supervise closely so the children don't handle breakable or hazardous items and so tiny fingers don't get pinched in the cupboard doors.) They can use the food to set up a grocery store on the kitchen table or the floor. Your shoppers will have fun selecting items, paying for them with play money, then loading and unloading them into and out of paper bags.

Baby

If your baby is older than six months, give him a few small food boxes to handle and stack. You also can create a small tower of boxes for him to knock over. If your baby is younger than six months, place him in his stroller for a walk around the grocery store to see the brightly colored items and watch his siblings bustle about. Also try crumpling a paper bag near him. He'll react to the interesting sound.

Toddler

Toddlers enjoy arranging objects, so let your toddler stock the shelves. Can he make a tower of soup cans? Can he sort the canned objects from the boxed ones? Sorting is an early mathematical skill.

Preschooler

Your preschooler can be a grocery store clerk. She can help locate food items, bag them, and then check out the customers. Provide her with some play money to use as change for her customers' transactions. Although she can't calculate exact change, she can imitate transactions she has witnessed at the real grocery store. Make sure she gives each customer a receipt (a Post-It Note) with either scribbles or handwritten numbers.

School-Age Child

Your school-age child can create a poster highlighting grocery store specials, using drawings or glued-on magazine cutouts of food. Have her work on the poster in the store so when customers walk by, she can inform them about the specials. Have her describe the items in enticing ways, such as "These green beans are fresh" or "This box of cereal has a toy inside it."

Parent Tip

The grocery store activity is a simple way to teach your children about charity and giving. While your children are "shopping," ask them each to pick out one or two items to place in a special bag that you have set aside. Tell them that you'll bring the bag to a local food shelf, where it can go to a family in need.

> My son and nephew used to spend hours unloading all the soup cans from my cabinet and arranging them on the table. They had just as much fun putting them all back!
>
> —Lisa

CHAPTER 3
Music & Movement

I remember watching my four-month-old son as he used all his strength to roll over for the first time. My husband and I waited eagerly, whispering encouraging words. He pushed, he struggled, and finally...success! He lifted up his head and gave a smile that seemed to say, "This is only the beginning!"

—Lisa

Sometimes it seems that kids' bodies have minds of their own, especially when they start hopping and bopping to music. In this chapter, we provide engaging activities and games that focus on physical movement or musical creations—often times both! Whether they're singing and dancing to their own music video, playing homemade instruments, or striking energizing yoga poses, your kids will have fun moving their bodies and appreciating music of all kinds.

Morning Stretches

Start your day with these energizing stretches!

What You'll Need	All Ages	Baby	Toddler	Preschooler	School-Age Child
Plush animals			✋	✋	✋

Sit with your children on the floor. Your toddler, preschooler, and school-age child will enjoy doing the stretches suggested below, and your baby will enjoy stretching with your help.

Baby

While your older children stretch, lay your baby on her back. Grasp one of her hands and her opposite foot. Gently stretch them out. Repeat this action with the other hand and foot. You can also try loosening up her hip muscles. In the same position, hold each of her legs and gently move them in a bicycling motion around and around.

Toddler, Preschooler, and School-Age Child

Show your older children how to do the following stretches:

- Hello, Sun Stretch: Sitting with your legs straight out in front of you, raise your arms above your head, then slowly reach for your feet.
- Out of Bed Bend: Sitting with your legs spread out to the sides, raise your arms above your head, then slowly bend to each side toward a foot.

- **Tickle Circle:** Sit in a circle with your legs straight out so your feet touch everyone else's. Reach forward and tickle one another's feet!

- **The Go-Go:** Find a partner, then sit facing each other with your legs straight out and your feet touching. Grab your partner's hands, then take turns leaning back while gently pulling your partner forward. If one partner is taller than the other, he will have to bend his legs while leaning forward.

- **The Up and About:** Stand up and hold a plush animal over your head. Bring the animal down to your toes, then stand back up and hold it straight out in front of you. Twist from side to side.

It's a Jungle Out There

This energetic activity will have your children crawling, hopping, and prancing like wild animals.

What You'll Need	All Ages	Baby	Toddler	Preschooler	School-Age Child
Hula-Hoops (or pillows)	✋				

Arrange a Hula-Hoop (or pillow) for each child on the floor, spacing them about two feet apart. As a family, choose a wild animal, then have your children pretend to be the animal and move like it around the Hula-Hoops. They may need to hop, slither on their bellies, or crawl on all fours. Explain to them that the Hula-Hoops are hiding places where they can go if there's danger. When you say, "I hear something! Hide!" they should move into the nearest Hula-Hoop, crouch low, and stay still until you say all is clear. Repeat the game with another animal.

Baby

Team up with your baby and hold her face-out as you move like the animal. She'll love the movement and watching the other "animals" in action. To help build her vocabulary, say to her, "We're pretending to be a *bear*."

Toddler

Animals have many ways of getting around—so does a toddler.
Your toddler may enjoy laying on the ground and slithering
like a snake or getting on all fours and strutting like a lion. If
he needs direction, point out how his siblings use their bodies
to move like animals. For example, you could point out how
his sister holds her hands on her hips and lifts one knee to
look like a flamingo.

Preschooler and School-Age Child

Encourage your preschooler and school-age child to act out
the motions of animals without naming them. Can anyone
in the family guess what they are? If not, they can give clues
such as "This animal has a very long neck." Once someone
recognizes the animal, everyone can act out its movements.

Shake It

Your children will get in the groove with these homemade
make-'em-and-shake-'em percussion instruments.

What You'll Need	All Ages	Baby	Toddler	Preschooler	School-Age Child
Empty containers with lids, such as plastic bottles, plastic tubs, shoeboxes, coffee cans, and so on	🖐				
Rattling materials, such as dried beans, pebbles, uncooked rice, dry cereal, cotton balls, marbles, and coins	🖐				
Masking tape	🖐				
Spoons				🖐	🖐

Give your children empty containers with lids, such as plastic
bottles, plastic tubs, small shoeboxes, coffee cans, and so on.
Have them pour dried beans, pebbles, or other rattling materials
into them, then help them secure the lids with tape. Then let
them shake away, making their own rhythms or following the
beat of their favorite music! *Note:* Supervise closely because
the small rattling materials could pose a choking risk for
younger children.

Baby

Make an instrument for your baby with a container that will
be easy to grasp, such as a plastic bottle. He'll love making
noise on his own. If he's not able to hold the instrument,
shake it close to him and move it slowly around him. He may
follow it with his eyes as well as his ears.

Toddler

Have your toddler pick a container and a rattling material,
then fill her container for her. She can help secure the lid on
the container, though, if you put pieces of tape on the edge of
a table for her to peel off and stick. This simple task will challenge her budding motor skills, as will shaking the instrument
when it's finished.

Preschooler and School-Age Child

Let your older children experiment by filling different containers with different rattling materials to hear the different
sounds they make. Have them look around the house for big
and small containers made from plastic, cardboard, and wood.
Encourage them to fill the containers with uncooked rice, dry
cereal, cotton balls, marbles, or coins. They can also try banging on their instruments with spoons instead of shaking them.

Pick a Move

This activity combines chance with imagination in order to get your family moving!

What You'll Need	All Ages	Baby	Toddler	Preschooler	School-Age Child
Deck of playing cards	✋				
Watch or clock	✋				

Remove the face cards from a deck of playing cards. Have your children sit on the floor in a circle and place the remaining cards face-down in the center. Have the first player choose a movement—like hopping on one foot, running in place, skipping, doing jumping jacks, crawling, or twirling around—then have her pick a card. The number on the card indicates how many seconds she must do the movement. For instance, if she chooses to do jumping jacks and picks a nine card, she must do jumping jacks for nine seconds. Use a watch or clock to time her, or teach your children to time seconds by counting, "One Mississippi, two Mississippi…" and so on. When she's done, the next player thinks of a movement and picks a card.

Baby

Your baby can do this activity, too. When it's his turn, have his siblings choose a movement and a card for him. Then help him walk, crawl, roll, or jump for the appropriate number of seconds. Have his siblings count each second aloud as a way to make it even more exciting.

Toddler

Suggest a movement you know your toddler can do, or if she has something in mind she would like to try, let her go for it! Let her pick a card and then count to that number together. If she draws a three, announce, "[Toddler's name] is going to show us how she can roll. She will roll for three seconds. Are you ready, [toddler's name]?" Have her siblings count the seconds as she performs.

Preschooler and School-Age Child

Encourage your preschooler and school-age child to demonstrate moves they learned at school or in a class. For example, they may choose to tap dance or pretend to ice-skate. To make it a bit more challenging, ask your children to do their movements with their eyes closed or in a circle.

> My preschooler loved when he picked a ten. Doing the movement for ten seconds while his siblings cheered him on was really fun for him!
>
> —Lisa

Give Me an A!

Bring letters to life with this body-twisting activity.

What You'll Need	All Ages	Baby	Toddler	Preschooler	School-Age Child
Poster board	✋				
Marker	✋				
Blanket		✋			

Before doing this activity, write the alphabet in capital letters on a sheet of poster board. Tell your children they can use it as a visual cue to help them shape their bodies into letters.

Baby

Lay your baby on a blanket and closely supervise as her siblings work to form a letter with her body. For instance, they can raise her arms wide above her head and hold her legs together to make a *Y*. Or they can team up with her to make a letter, such as if the baby and a sibling lie at angles and touch toes to create a *V*. If your baby is too young or just restless during the letter-building attempts, sit her close the chart and point to the letters as her siblings make each one with their bodies.

Toddler

Your toddler may be starting to visually recognize letters. This activity will re-emphasize the shapes of the letters he knows. Point to letters with simple, continuous lines, like *I* or *C*. Help him create these lines by standing him up straight like the *I* or helping him move his body and arms into the curve of the *C*.

Preschooler and School-Age Child

Your preschooler and school-age child can look at the chart and choose which letters to form individually, as a pair, or with the help of other family members. Can they come up with a formation for every letter? Let them use their imagination and team skills to tackle the challenge.

Parent Tip
Take pictures of your children as they form letters, especially the letters in your family name.

Pop! Go Our Bodies

Gather around in a circle for a fun game that will have your children popping and singing.

What You'll Need	All Ages	Baby	Toddler	Preschooler	School-Age Child
Bodies and voices!	✋				

Hold hands and walk in a circle as you sing these lyrics to the tune of "Pop! Goes the Weasel." For each round, choose two children to name.

All around [child's name's] house,
[sibling's name] is watching.
(S)he shouts "Boo!" (The child named in the first line shouts "Boo!")
We count to two. (Everyone counts to two and crouches close to the ground.)
Pop! go our bodies! (Release hands and everyone pops up, twirls, then drops down.)

Baby

If your baby is younger than eight months old, hold her in your arms as you walk. If she is older, support her under her arms and help her walk around in a circle. The activity will be great walking practice, and the song will reinforce her knowledge of family members' names. She'll love to hear her own name, too.

Toddler, Preschooler, and School-Age Child

Encourage your toddler, preschooler, and school-age child
to make special moves when it's time to pop. Let them create
their own moves at first, but then teach them these fun
jumping motions:

- **The Straight Jump:** Keep your body and legs as straight
  as possible as you jump in the air and land again.
- **The Tuck Jump:** Touch your hands to your knees
  while jumping.
- **The Straddle Jump:** Jump up and spread your legs apart.

We've Got the Beat

Create beats that everyone can move to!

What You'll Need	All Ages	Baby	Toddler	Preschooler	School-Age Child
Spoon and pot	✋				
Rattle toys		✋			

Have each of your children take a turn creating a beat with their hands, feet, or a spoon and pot while everyone else dances and moves to it. Tell them to freeze when the beat stops and move faster when the beat does.

Baby

Your baby is learning to locate the source of noises. He may turn his head to track the sound of the beat. He may also move his arms and bounce to the rhythm with or without your help. If your baby is six months or older, he may enjoy making noise by shaking his rattle toys. Help him shake a toy to a beat his siblings can move to.

Toddler

Reinforce how your toddler's body should move to the beat by saying, "The beat is very, very slow. Move your body slowly." Or "This beat is fast. Shake your body to the beat. Shake it fast!" Put your hands gently on his shoulders if he needs help remembering to freeze whenever the beat stops! When it is his turn to make the beat for his siblings, prompt him to slow down, speed up, and stop at various times.

Preschooler and School-Age Child

Encourage your preschooler and school-age child to get creative with their movements. When the beat is a loud, slow banging, they may want to dance like giants. When the beat has quick, soft sounds, they may want to crawl like ants. Connecting sounds to animals or objects will boost their imaginations. When it is their turn to create the beat, perhaps they will do it to the beat of a familiar song or nursery rhyme.

> I play this game with my older children in the morning when I'm trying to get their shoes and coats on. They put their things on to my beat. If the beat is slow, they move slowly when zipping their coat up. When my beat is fast, they race to get their shoes on.
>
> —Lisa

Act It Out

Encourage your children to act out simple nursery rhymes and children's songs.

What You'll Need	All Ages	Baby	Toddler	Preschooler	School-Age Child
Nursery rhyme books or CDs	👋				

Using books or CDs that feature nursery rhymes, help your children find rhymes that inspire movement, such as "Jack Be Nimble" or "Jack and Jill." As you recite the rhymes out loud together (or play the CD), encourage them to add the coordinating actions.

Baby

Have fun moving with your baby to the nursery rhymes. For example, lift her up or down for "The Itsy-Bitsy Spider" and playfully lower her to one side for "I'm a Little Teapot."

Toddler

Your toddler may follow the motions you make with your baby or those his older siblings make. Be sure to pick a few familiar rhymes he knows, and perhaps say them slowly line by line so he has time to make each action.

Preschooler and School-Age Child

Have your preschooler and school-age child partner up whenever possible, like in "Row, Row, Row Your Boat." They can face one another and hold hands as they lean forward and backward as in a rowing motion. You may also want them to leaf through the nursery rhyme book and pick one or two new ones to teach their family, complete with movements to depict what is happening in the rhyme.

Did You Know?

The origins of most nursery rhymes reflect events in history. "Jack Be Nimble" is thought to be associated with the old tradition of candle leaping, which used to be featured at English fairs.

Soaring with Scarves

Use silk scarves to get your kids' minds and bodies moving.

What You'll Need	All Ages	Baby	Toddler	Preschooler	School-Age Child
Silk (or cotton) scarves (available at your local craft store)	🖐				
Music	🖐				

Give each child a scarf, turn on some music, and let them use their imaginations to move their bodies and their scarves however they want. Change the song every thirty seconds and have them slow down or speed up their movements, depending on how the song makes them feel.

Baby

Dance with baby in your arms. If she's older than six months, she may enjoy holding the scarf in her hands and waving it. If she's younger, hold the scarf near her face and move it to the beat of the music.

Toddler

Encourage your toddler to try new movements with his scarf, such as holding it low to the ground or high to the sky. You can also have him twirl with his scarf, or show him how to scrunch his scarf into a ball and throw it into the air. Can he catch it as it drifts back to the ground?

Preschooler

Your preschooler won't likely need any instruction as she skips or gallops with the scarf to fast music. During a slower song, though, have her try this relaxing technique: Have her hold the scarf in front of her face, take a deep breath in, and then exhale to blow the scarf up.

School-Age Child

While dancing, your school-age child can have fun swirling his scarf in front of him in the shape of a circle. Can he form the letters of his name? For example, he can move the scarf quickly down and to the right to make an *L*?

Yoga

Yoga is a great way to help kids of all ages focus and relax.

What You'll Need	All Ages	Baby	Toddler	Preschooler	School-Age Child
Bath towels	✋				

In a room with a lot of open space, show your children how to do the yoga poses on page 96. Because the Cobra and Child's Pose require lying on the floor, it's best to do this activity in a carpeted room. If the floor isn't carpeted, have the children do these poses on a bath towel. Below you'll find some age-appropriate ways your children can enjoy these yoga poses. *Note:* Many communities offer yoga classes for children. If your children enjoy this activity, check for classes in your area.

Baby

Even a young baby can enjoy yoga! If your baby can lift his head, lay him on his belly and watch him move into a version of the Cobra pose as he raises his head and shoulders. (If he's not yet able to lift his head, his body will still benefit from the tummy time.)While your older children practice the Down Dog pose, your baby will enjoy looking up at their upside-down faces as he sits or lies on his back nearby.

Aquapella

Drip, *drop*, *plish*, *plosh*, *burble*, *babble*—your kids can create "music" with water!

What You'll Need	All Ages	Baby	Toddler	Preschooler	School-Age Child
Towels	🖐				
Baking pan		🖐			
Plastic cup			🖐		
Drinking straw			🖐		
Drinking glasses				🖐	
Metal spoon				🖐	
Plastic bottles					🖐

Tell your children they're going to make "music" with water, and they'll each play a different "instrument." Do this activity in your kitchen, where you can find all the materials and you won't have to worry about making a mess. (You still might want to keep some towels handy, though.)

Baby

If your baby is six months or older, pour about an inch of water in a baking pan and place it on the highchair tray. Encourage her to slap the water. It won't be long until she's splashing and creating her own unique percussion sound. If your baby is younger than six months, guide her hands to help her slap the water.

Toddler

Fill a plastic cup halfway with water and give your toddler a straw. Show him how to blow into the water with the straw to create bubbles and a silly sound. (You may need to remind him that while it's fun to do this "musical technique" now, it's not something he should do every time he drinks from a straw!)

Preschooler

Help your preschooler fill three glasses with water: one glass almost to the top, the second halfway, and the third with only a bit. Place the glasses on a table. Your preschooler can gently tap the side of each glass with a metal spoon. Note how the sound changes in each glass, depending on how much water they hold. Which one makes the highest sound? Maybe he'll be able to play a simple tune like "Mary Had a Little Lamb" while he taps the glasses.

School-Age Child

Have your school-age child fill three plastic bottles with varying levels of water. Show her how to make music by perching her lips on the edge of the bottle opening and blowing gently. Have her blow into all three and note how the sound changes. If you have different-size bottles, have her experiment with their sound, too.

New Musical Chairs

We've taken the competitiveness out of this traditional game
and added more fun.

What You'll Need	All Ages	Baby	Toddler	Preschooler	School-Age Child
Chairs (one for each child)	🖐				
Tape	🖐				
Photos (one of each child)	🖐				

Set up the chairs back to back in an open area. Tape one of your
children's photos to each chair. Sing a song of your choice to
start everyone walking or dancing around the chairs. When
you yell "Stop!" each child must hurry to sit on the chair with
his respective photo. After a few rounds, change the order of
the chairs or the photos.

Baby

Sway and move to the beat of your song as you march around
with your baby in your arms. Feeling your movement and
hearing you sing is a great way for her to experience the joy
of music. When you say "Stop!" your baby will enjoy the
hustle and bustle of everyone scrambling for their chairs.

Toddler

Encourage your toddler to make silly movements as he goes around the chairs. Can he jump, tiptoe, or trot? Can he move slowly or quickly to match the beat of your song? When it's time to find his chair, he may end up waiting to see which chair is empty after his siblings have found their places. To help him understand that the photos designate each child's chair, point to his photo and say, "Who is that? Whose chair is this?"

Preschooler and School-Age Child

Challenge your older children to think of other fun rules for this new version of musical chairs. Perhaps they'll suggest you arrange the chairs farther apart, or perhaps they'll tape the photos face-down so players must lift them one by one to find their chairs.

Pop Stars

Have aspiring pop stars in your household? You and your
family can perform your own music videos!

What You'll Need	All Ages	Baby	Toddler	Preschooler	School-Age Child
Favorite music	🖐				
Dress-up clothes, such as hats and scarves	🖐				
"Microphones," such as spoons, toothbrushes, hairbrushes, and so on	🖐				
Camcorder or other recording device	🖐				

Play your children's favorite music or ask them to sing a song
for you. Give them pretend microphones, and encourage them
to dress up using hats, scarves, or other fun clothes. Each child
can take a turn singing, humming, or cooing into a microphone
as if a pop star performing in a music video or concert. If possible, capture the performance with a camcorder or other
recording device, then watch or listen to it as a family.

Baby

No doubt, the sound of your voices is one of your baby's favorite
things, so he'll love to listen to everyone sing. But make sure
he gets in on the action, too. If he tries to gurgle or make
sounds, mimic them back to him. He'll enjoy this interaction.

During the performance, he can be center stage while one of his siblings helps him dance.

Toddler

Your toddler may be happy simply blowing into the microphone, or she may be ready to sing a few notes of her favorite song. Remind her of the lyrics by singing a few words then pausing to let her guess what comes next. See if she will finish the lyric after a few tries!

Preschooler and School-Age Child

Let your older children take the lead with the performance. Encourage them to choose a song and help their siblings learn the words. They may even want to make up a dance routine or body movements to go along with the song.

> My children love to perform. My job is to introduce them. I make a big deal out of it, saying, "And now, ladies and gentlemen, I would like to introduce the amazingly talented Kyle and the beautiful, sensational Brooke!" They get a kick out of it and perform their little hearts out!
> —Heather

Little Gymnasts

Get your kids moving with balancing, jumping, and tumbling exercises!

What You'll Need	All Ages	Baby	Toddler	Preschooler	School-Age Child
Exercise mats (or a mattress)	🖐				
Bath towel		🖐			
Masking tape			🖐		

Below you'll find some age-appropriate gymnastics for your children. Be sure to supervise closely and use exercise mats (or a mattress) for safety.

Baby

Here's a fun "floor exercise" for babies at least three months old: Lay her on her back on a mat or bath towel and encourage her to reach for her toes. Put bright-colored socks on her feet and slowly raise them up so they are in her view. Can she reach for them?

Toddler

Help your toddler do a logroll: Have him lie horizontally across the mat with his arms straight over his head so he looks like a log. Encourage him to roll to the end of the mat in this position. Also, place a few X marks with masking tape about one foot apart on the floor. Suggest that your toddler try to jump from one to another.

Preschooler

Help your preschooler do a forward somersault on the mat. Show him how to squat with his hands on the mat in front of him. Have him tuck his head as if he's looking at his bellybutton, then tell him to use his legs to push up into a roll.

School-Age Child

Teach your school-age child how to do a handstand. Slide the mat close to a wall. Have her face the wall and place her hands palms down on the mat. Help her kick her legs up against the wall. Proper position requires that she lock her knees and arms, point her toes, and tuck in her neck. Be sure to supervise closely.

Dancing with Feeling

Let your children express themselves with some creative dance moves!

What You'll Need	All Ages	Baby	Toddler	Preschooler	School-Age Child
Variety of music	✋				

In a large, open space, play a variety of music, like big band, classical, pop, country, and lullabies. While the music plays, call out different feelings such as "Happy!" or "Sad!" and encourage your children to express each of those feelings through dance. If they need direction, here are some examples:

- Sad: Slump your shoulders and make a sad face.
- Happy: Throw your arms in the air and grin.
- Sneaky: Tiptoe or creep slowly.
- Frustrated: Stomp your feet and yell.
- Silly: Spin in circles and make funny faces.
- Excited: Make quick twists and turns.
- Sleepy: Make slow, drawn-out movements.

Baby

Your baby will enjoy the movement and music as you dance while holding him. Babies love to study faces, so be sure to make exaggerated expressions for each feeling. He may try to mimic you!

Toddler

Expressing himself through dance will reinforce the different emotions your toddler is beginning to identify. To get him started, ask, "What does it feel like to be happy? Do you feel like jumping up and down?" or "What do you feel like doing when you're sleepy? Do you rub your eyes?" Demonstrate the movements and encourage him to join in. He may also watch his siblings and mirror their movements.

Preschooler

Your preschooler may discover that dance is a good way to communicate feelings she has trouble expressing in words. For example, she may find it difficult to express anger or sadness. Encourage her to come up with different dance moves to express those feelings in appropriate ways.

School-Age Child

Have your school-age child call out a few feelings for everyone to dance to. Challenge her to listen to the music and identify a feeling that matches its tone and mood. Does a country ballad sound sad? Does a big band tune feel cheerful?

Bounce to the Beat

This activity will challenge your kids' balance as they bounce to the beat!

What You'll Need	All Ages	Baby	Toddler	Preschooler	School-Age Child
Medium-size balls (about 12 inches in diameter)			🖐	🖐	🖐
Exercise ball		🖐			
Music	🖐				

In a large, open space, have your toddler, preschooler, and school-age child each sit on a ball. Play a variety of music with different tempos, and challenge your children to keep their balance as they bounce to the beats. You can join in, too, by bouncing on an exercise ball while holding your baby.

Baby

Hold your baby while you sit on an exercise ball. (If you don't have one, hold her on your lap as you sit on a chair.) If she is younger than four months, face her toward you and hold her so her head is over your shoulder. If she is older and has more neck control, hold her face out so she can see her siblings. Bounce to the beat of the music. The action will stimulate a calming reflex that may put her right to sleep!

Toddler

Keeping his balance on the ball will be a new challenge for your toddler. To help him practice balancing, have him sit on his ball near a wall he can use as support. If he needs more assistance, hold him under his arms as he sits on the ball, and raise and lower his body to create the bouncing effect. Make sure to bounce fast during an upbeat tempo and slow for a gentle rhythm.

Preschooler and School-Age Child

For an additional challenge, see if your preschooler and school-age child can clap their hands or slap their knees while bouncing. It will be harder than they think! Because they are growing tall, their legs will have to bend closely to their torsos in order to stay on the ball.

Invisible Baseball

You won't need any equipment for this fun movement game!

What You'll Need	All Ages	Baby	Toddler	Preschooler	School-Age Child
Imaginations!	✋				

In an open space, tell your children it's baseball time, but you're going to play with invisible equipment! Everyone— even the baby—can participate. Take some time to teach your older children the playing techniques below, but you may need to help your younger children make the motions. For each turn, assign a pitcher, batter, and fielders, depending on the number of players. Encourage your children to play a game, and cheer on their pretend plays!

Pitching
Have the pitcher pretend she's holding a baseball in her hands. Her fingers and thumbs should be stretched out and curved around the ball. Teach her to make an overhand throw by pulling her throwing arm back with elbow bent, then springing it forward as she releases the ball.

Batting
It takes a lot of practice to hold a bat, let alone swing it, so this a great way to get ready for real baseball. Have the batter pretend to hold a bat by lining up his knuckles on the handle with his dominant hand on top. He can stand sideways on home

plate with his head facing forward, hold the bat behind his shoulders, and swing out in front of him as the pitch approaches. After a hit, your child can run the bases. (You can set up some checkpoints for the bases or simply let him run in a circle.)

Fielding

Encourage the fielder to watch the batter closely to know when a hit is coming her way. Have her pretend to wear a mitt on her nondominant hand, stretching her fingers wide to open the mitt and closing the thumb to the fingers to catch the ball. Using her dominant hand, she can retrieve the ball from the mitt, then throw it to a base to stop the runner or throw it back to the pitcher.

Walk in My Steps

With this activity, your kids will understand what it means to walk in someone else's footsteps!

What You'll Need	All Ages	Baby	Toddler	Preschooler	School-Age Child
Felt (2 sheets per child)	✋				
Chalk	✋				
Music	✋				

To begin, have each child stand on a sheet of felt while you or an older child traces the footprints with chalk. (Hold the baby under her arms if she's not old enough to stand on her own.) Repeat on another sheet of felt so each child makes two sets of footprints. Encourage your children to place their feet in different positions for each tracing. They can point their feet outward or inward, stand with feet together or spread apart, position one foot above the other, or even stand on one foot. When you're done tracing, choose an open space on the floor and lay all the felt sheets in a long path. Turn on some lively music and have your children move from one set of footprints to the next, placing their feet in the proper positions.

Baby

If your baby isn't walking on her own yet, hold her under her arms or by the hands as she "walks" through the footprint path. She may not put her feet in the right positions, but she'll love taking her own steps. Otherwise, you can hold her in your arms as you walk and hop through the path, stepping to the music.

Toddler

Your toddler may try to speed through the path, but encourage her to take her time and study the position of each different set of footprints so she can match it. Say, "See how this foot points out and this foot points in? Can you put your feet that way, too?"

Preschooler

Add some arm movements to give your preschooler an extra challenge as he walks through the prints. Can he hold his hands above his head and clap to the beat of the music while stepping into the prints? This may also be a good time to practice telling left from right by having your preschooler say "Left!" or "Right!" as he puts each respective foot in a print.

School-Age Child

After everyone has a turn, put your school-age child in charge of arranging the felt pieces in a new path. He may want to shuffle the order of the footprints, make a circle or square with the pieces, or space them farther apart so he and his siblings need to jump from one to the other and land as the footprints dictate.

Clap! Snap! Stomp!

This noisy activity is a great way to channel your children's energy.

What You'll Need	All Ages	Baby	Toddler	Preschooler	School-Age Child
Bodies!	✋				

Teach your children the following chant and do the actions together:

Clap, clap, clap—my hands can do that part.
  (Clap hands in rhythm.)
Snap, snap, snap—my fingers are so fast.
  (Snap fingers in rhythm.)
Stomp, stomp, stomp—my feet can keep the beat.
  (Stomp feet in rhythm.)
La, la, la—do you hear me now?
  (Turn around in a circle.)

Next, call out one of your children's names and say, "Break it down!" That child gets to move and make sounds however he likes, then everyone else copies him. After a few seconds, say, "Freeze, please!" At that point, everyone must stand still and be quiet. Begin the chant again, choosing a different name next time for the "breakdown."

Baby

Your baby will enjoy doing the actions with your help. Hold your hands over his and bring them together to show him how to clap. If he's older than six months, he may love to clap by himself. Whether sitting or laying down, help him stomp by lifting his legs up and down. Don't forget to give the baby a turn to "break it down" and be the leader!

Toddler

Chances are, your toddler may need help learning how to snap. Hold your hands in front of him and snap in slow motion, showing him how the middle finger touches the top of the thumb and then slides down. Help position his fingers for a snap. Even if he doesn't make much of a sound, encourage his efforts!

Preschooler

Your preschooler will love this silly, noisy activity, so the challenge will be composing herself when it's time to be still and quiet. If necessary, touch her on the shoulder when you give the command to freeze.

School-Age Child

When it's her turn to be the leader for the breakdown, have your school-age child make sounds not with her voice, but with her body. She can slap her knees or rub the carpet with her feet. Encourage her to teach her siblings new movements to do.

Hokey-Pokey Family

Everyone can "shake it all about" in this fun variation of
a traditional tune!

What You'll Need	All Ages	Baby	Toddler	Preschooler	School-Age Child
The whole family!	✋				

Have your children stand in a circle. If your baby can stand
with support, help him join the circle. Otherwise, hold him as
you stand in the circle. Sing "The Hokey-Pokey" as a family,
replacing each verse's body part with a child's name. For
example, if your toddler's name is Emily, sing:

We put Emily in. (She runs into the middle of the circle.)
We put Emily out. (She runs back to her spot in the circle.)
We put Emily in. (She runs into the middle of the circle.)
And she shakes it all about. (She shakes her whole body.)
We do the hokey-pokey, and we turn ourselves around.
    (Everyone turns around in a circle.)
That's what it's all about! (Everyone claps to the beat of
    each word.)

Repeat the song, using each sibling's name. When it's the baby's
turn, hold him as you move in and out of the circle, and gently
sway from side to side when it's time to "shake." Make sure
you take a turn, too. After everyone has had a turn, repeat the
song once more, using "the whole family" as the subject!

Ring Those Bells

Your children will enjoy making these bell wands, but they'll really love conducting their very own bell choir!

What You'll Need	All Ages	Baby	Toddler	Preschooler	School-Age Child
Paper towel tubes	🖐				
Paint or crayons	🖐				
Clear contact paper		🖐			
Hole punch	🖐				
Various craft bells (2 per child)	🖐				
Yarn	🖐				

Give your toddler, preschooler, and school-age child each a paper-towel tube to decorate with paint and crayons. Have them decorate a tube for your baby as well. Wrap the baby's decorated tube in clear contact paper in case she mouths it. Punch a small hole at both ends of each tube, then tie a bell to each hole with yarn. If you use different styles and sizes of bells, your bell choir will have a variety of tones.

Once the bell wands are complete, each child can take a turn as the conductor. He can stand in front and point to a sibling when he wants her to ring her bells.

Baby

The bell wand is perfect for a baby just learning to grasp objects. Let her shake it to hear the bells. When it's her turn to be the conductor, sit her on your lap and move her arms to point to her siblings. After a few tries, see if she'll swing her arms on her own. Prompt your older children to play whenever they see her move. She'll love realizing that her siblings ring the bells according to her movements!

Toddler

Your toddler will enjoy standing in front of his siblings and pointing to the bells he wants to hear. Depending on how fast he points, he can control the tempo of his choir. Encourage him to move his arms fast when he wants the bells to ring quickly and move his arms slowly when he wants them to slow down.

Preschooler

How can your preschooler make her bells ring besides shaking the wand? Can she tap the bells with her fingers or roll the wand back and forth on the ground? Have her pick a new technique, teach it to the choir, then lead them in a performance.

School-Age Child

Encourage your school-age child to perform a solo of a simple tune such as "Jingle Bells" or "Mary Had a Little Lamb." As an extra challenge, have her conduct the choir to create a specific tune together. She may want to sing the song as she points to each sibling, helping them follow the tune.

CHAPTER 4

Outdoor Adventures

I happily take my kids outside every chance I get. Where else can they burn off energy, make a mess, and discover countless new things? We stomp in rain puddles, follow tracks in the snow, and study clouds for dinosaurs and cars.

—Lisa

There's a world of fun for you and your kids just outside your door. In this chapter, we include classic and new outdoor games that are fun for every age group. We also include a variety of special experiences kids can have only outdoors, such as searching for nature's treasures, studying the stars and clouds, and getting soaked with the sprinkler. The only hard part may be getting your children to come back inside after a long day of playing and exploring!

Strollin' through Nature

Help your children explore and collect natural treasures.

What You'll Need	All Ages	Baby	Toddler	Preschooler	School -Age Child
Paper bags			🖐	🖐	🖐
Glue stick				🖐	
Construction paper				🖐	
Markers				🖐	
Binoculars					🖐
Notebook and pencil					🖐

Give your toddler, preschooler, and school-age child each a paper bag, then take a walk through your neighborhood or a park. Have your children use the bags to collect nature items, like flowers, rocks, and pinecones.

Baby
Nature provides a world of stimulation for your baby. Talk to her about your surroundings. Point out a colorful flower, a smooth rock, or chirping birds. Encourage your other children to describe what they see to her as well.

Toddler
Your toddler will love picking up items and dropping them in his bag. Help build his vocabulary by identifying what he puts

in his bag. For example, say, "You found a green leaf. Can you say 'green leaf?'"

Preschooler

Describe an object in your preschooler's sight and have him guess what it is. For example, say, "I spy something green" to describe grass. Feel free to give him plenty of hints. He can take a turn describing an object and having you or his siblings guess what it is. When you get home, help him glue his nature finds onto a large sheet of construction paper. If you like, help him identify and label each object.

School-Age Child

Your school-age child can use a pair of binoculars to "collect" sightings of nature objects out of normal sight, like a bird in a treetop or a butterfly on the far side of a field. If you like, give her a notebook to record what she observes on your walk.

Parent Tip
To prepare for your nature walk, take a trip to your local library and check out nature guides on your area.

Ball In, Out, and About

This silly game will bring some music and action to your outdoor time.

What You'll Need	All Ages	Baby	Toddler	Preschooler	School-Age Child
Hula-Hoop (or two)	✋				
Foam balls	✋				
Marker			✋		

Lay a Hula-Hoop on the ground and have your kids sit around it. Give each child a foam ball of any size. Sing the following song to the tune of "The Hokey-Pokey" and follow the indicated movements:

You put the ball in the circle.
  (Hold the ball to the ground inside the Hula-Hoop.)
And you take the ball right out.
  (Hold the ball outside the Hula-Hoop.)
You put the ball in the circle.
  (Hold the ball inside the Hula-Hoop.)
And you shake it all about.
  (Shake the ball as hard as you can.)
We do the bally-bally (Stand up.)
And we give the ball a throw (Throw the ball in the air.)
Hey, ball, where did you go? (Chase the ball.)

Have your children run to collect their balls and gather back around the Hula-Hoop as quickly as they can.

Baby

Partner with your baby for this activity. If she is six months or older, give her an easy-to-grasp ball and guide her through the movements. She'll soon anticipate the actions and may try to release the ball on cue. Applaud her efforts! If your baby is younger, hold her while you perform the actions. She'll enjoy the movement and the song.

Toddler

It won't take many rounds until your toddler joins in the movements and belts out some of the song lyrics. Make her ball extra special: Use a marker to draw a smiley face on both sides. This way, she can practice her tracking skills and find her ball quickly as it rolls away.

Preschooler and School-Age Child

To challenge your preschooler and school-age child, place another Hula-Hoop on the ground about five feet away from the first one. When it's time to toss their balls into the air, they can aim for the second Hula-Hoop. This exercise is a good precursor to skills required to play basketball and baseball. Your preschooler and school-age child can also try to catch their balls after they throw them in the air.

Sand Discoveries

Sand has a wonderful texture that most children love to have running through their fingertips or squishing between their toes. Let your children experiment with sand using different items.

What You'll Need	All Ages	Baby	Toddler	Preschooler	School-Age Child
Sandbox	🖐				
Sand toys, such as funnels, shovels, and pails			🖐	🖐	🖐
Clear plastic bottle		🖐			
Rocks or small sticks					🖐

Set up a sandbox for your children outside, then have them use different objects to play with the sand. (If you don't have a sandbox, you can make one by adding sand—available at landscaping centers—to a large kiddie pool. Or you can use a sandbox at a local park.)

Baby

Babies love to discover new textures. If your baby is younger than six months, trickle a little sand from your hand over her hand. (Make sure none gets in her mouth.) If she is older, half-fill a clear plastic bottle with sand, close it tightly, and let her shake it, roll it, and turn it upside down to watch the sand move.

Toddler

Hold a funnel over a pail and show your toddler how to fill the funnel with sand by using a shovel or a cup. He will enjoy watching the sand drain into the pail. You also can give him a small amount of water to mix with the sand to see how the consistency changes.

Preschooler

Show your preschooler how to make a tower by filling a pail with sand, packing it down, and quickly flipping it over on the ground. Challenge her to build a sand castle by making towers next to each other.

School-Age Child

Your school-age child may enjoy setting up a sand town with roads, rivers, mountains, and bridges. He can use rocks to outline a road or small sticks to create a bridge. If he likes, he can make a "drip castle": After he's built a sand castle, show him how to make a loose fist with one hand then slowly pour a little wet sand through it and onto the sides of the sand castle. The water will make the sand "glob" together, creating a cool texture!

Welcome to Water World

This water play activity is perfect for a warm day.

What You'll Need	All Ages	Baby	Toddler	Preschooler	School-Age Child
Bowls or buckets	✋				
Water "tools," such as sponges, ladles, funnels, spoons, paintbrushes, spray bottles, rocks, and measuring cups	✋				

Go outside and fill a small bowl or bucket with water for each child. Then let them explore what they can do with the water!

Baby

Position your baby near her bowl of water. If she is six months or older, dip a ladle in the water and show her how to fill and empty it. If your baby is younger, let her see and hear water pouring into the bowl, feel water sprinkling on her hands, and taste a drop of water in her mouth.

Toddler

Your toddler's sense of discovery makes water play exciting. Let him experiment with a colander, funnel, or even a plastic cup with several holes poked on the bottom. Show him how to fill the objects with water and watch it drain out.

Preschooler

It will be fun for your preschooler to discover that water can move in different ways. Fill a small spray bottle. How far can he get the stream of water to reach? Mark the distance with a small rock and have him try again. Later, fill a large bowl with some water and give him a paintbrush or large spoon to stir in a circular motion. How fast can he get the water to swirl? After he stops stirring, how long does the water continue to move?

School-Age Child

Sharpen your school-age child's measuring and predicting skills. Have her predict the number of cups it'll take to fill her bowl, then see if she's right. Then have her predict the number of rocks she can add to her bowl of water before the water overflows. At the end of the activity, have your school-age child refill her bowl and set it someplace where it won't be disturbed. Ask her to predict how much water will be left in the bowl after a week has passed.

Stargazing

On a clear summer night, head outside with your family to view the sky.

What You'll Need	All Ages	Baby	Toddler	Preschooler	School-Age Child
Large blanket	🖐				
Celestial map or book on constellations					🖐
Flashlight					🖐
Red tissue paper					🖐

Find a spot to stargaze, whether it be your own backyard or a public park. Avoid sitting directly under streetlights. The farther you are from city lights, the more you'll see. (If you can't find a starry enough sky, modify this activity into a visit to a planetarium.) Spread a large blanket for your family as you stargaze. There are approximately five thousand stars visible to the naked eye, and your children will love to talk about those they see.

Baby

The stars may be too dim for your baby to see, but she'll enjoy listening to her family talk and the nature sounds. Lay her on her back with her siblings. Point to the stars and talk with her about all the nighttime noises she hears.

Toddler

Your toddler will find an outdoor nighttime activity exciting! If the moon is out, ask him if he can point to the brightest object in the sky. Entice his imagination by asking if he can see the "man in the moon" and what he may be doing up there. Also hold his hand to point to the stars and count them together.

Preschooler

Help your preschooler find a few popular stars and constellations, like the North Star (Polaris) and the Big Dipper (part of Ursa Major). Tell her the stories behind the constellation names (which may require some research beforehand). Encourage her to find her own constellations and create stories about them.

School-Age Child

Your school-age child will enjoy using a celestial map to identify a constellation. To help him see the stars in the book without obscuring his siblings' view of the night sky, have him place red tissue paper over his flashlight.

Did You Know?
On the moon, it's three times as hot during the day and three times as cold at night than it is on Earth.

Hungry Wolf

How hungry is the wolf? Your kids will be tempted to find out during this action-packed game.

What You'll Need	All Ages	Baby	Toddler	Preschooler	School-Age Child
Hungry wolves!	✋				

Each child will have a turn playing the wolf. The wolf should stand with his back to the others. The rest of your children will stand in a line facing the wolf about thirty feet away. Each child will take a turn asking the wolf, "Mr. Wolf, what time is it?" The wolf will respond with any time he chooses. If he says "One o'clock," each child moves one step. If he says "Nine o'clock," each child moves nine steps forward. He can also reply at any time with, "It's lunchtime!" At that point, the players must run back to their starting places before the wolf reaches them.

Baby

Your baby will love to be in your arms during this game. Make sure you count the steps out loud as you move. Expect squeals and smiles as everyone rushes back when the wolf says it's lunchtime!

Toddler

Watch your toddler as he begins to anticipate the moves of this game. He may jump with anticipation when he hears, "It's lunchtime!" When it's his turn to be the wolf, you can either prompt him to say a certain time or give him two times to choose from.

Preschooler

Instead of taking steps, your preschooler can challenge herself by hopping on one foot or jumping with both. Tell her to choose a mode that's fast enough to escape the hungry wolf!

School-Age Child

Your school-age child is able to associate the time of day with various activities. When it's his turn to play wolf, encourage him to provide a time and a corresponding action. For instance, he may respond, "It's eight o'clock, and time to get dressed." He could even act out the motions, too!

The Backyard Parade

March to your own beat as your kids create a family marching band!

What You'll Need	All Ages	Baby	Toddler	Preschooler	School-Age Child
Plastic bucket and stick			✋	✋	✋
Plastic bottle with pebbles			✋	✋	✋
Plastic plates			✋	✋	✋
Paper towel tube			✋	✋	✋
Spoons		✋			
Old T-shirt				✋	
Sticks				✋	✋

Help your children make musical instruments from items around the house. They can make a drum from a bucket and a stick; a maraca from a plastic bottle filled with pebbles; cymbals from two plastic plates; or a trumpet, flute, or clarinet from a paper-towel tube. Then your children can parade around your yard, playing their makeshift instruments.

Baby

Your baby can be a member of the band, too. If he is around six months old, he may enjoy tapping two spoons together as you push him in his stroller. If he is younger, he will enjoy watching his siblings march and listening to them play.

Toddler

You or an older child can show your toddler how to march. Encourage her to lift her knees up high while she plays a drum or a maraca.

Preschooler

Do you have a flag your preschooler can wave in time with the marching band? If not, he can create a quick-and-easy flag tying an old T-shirt around the end of a stick.

School-Age Child

Your school-age child probably knows more songs than his siblings. Have him teach them a tune to march to, like "London Bridge," or call out a made-up title for a song they can create together with their instruments. He can lead the band, using a stick as a baton to help keep the tempo.

Parent Tip
For additional ideas for making home-made instruments for your marching band, see "Shake It" (page 80) and "Ring Those Bells" (page 116).

Green, Yellow, Red Lights

Your kids will be revving their engines during this back-yard game.

What You'll Need	All Ages	Baby	Toddler	Preschooler	School-Age Child
Moving bodies!	🖐				

Go out to the yard and explain the rules to your children: You will be the traffic light, and they will be the drivers. Designate a road, such as around the perimeter of the yard or from one end of the driveway to the other. Begin by saying "Green light," which means the drivers must take off (that is, run) along the road. When you say "Yellow light," they must drive slowly, preparing to stop. But when you say "Red light," the drivers must freeze. If a driver takes one step after a red light is called, he gets a ticket. The first ticket is a "warning," and the second ticket requires the driver to sit out until the next game. Continue the game until the last driver on the road wins.

Baby

Fasten your baby in a stroller and let an older sibling carefully drive him around for a few thrilling rounds! Or hold him in your arms and let him be the traffic light with you. Watching his siblings run around him will be just as exciting.

Toddler

Take a few extra minutes to teach your toddler about the meaning of green, yellow, and red lights, so she can follow along during the game. You or an older child may need to prompt her to run quickly, slow down, and stop until she gets the hang of it.

Preschooler

Your preschooler will love to make engine rumbles and brake screeches as a driver. He may get caught up in driving, so make sure he understands that a yellow light is a warning that a stop is coming very soon. Can he stop quickly enough?

School-Age Child

For fun, your school-age child can drive in reverse: Have her run backward down the road! Just tell her to look out for her siblings traveling in the other direction.

Sunflower, Shine for Me

Teach your children the joy of planting a flower and watching it grow!

What You'll Need	All Ages	Baby	Toddler	Preschooler	School-Age Child
Sunflower seeds	🖐				
Nesting cups or plastic bowls or cups		🖐			
Watering cans	🖐				
Hand shovels			🖐	🖐	🖐
Small pot			🖐		
Rock			🖐		
Journal or camera				🖐	🖐

When there's no longer danger of frost, pick a sunny open area in your yard. Your children can have fun learning how to plant and tend sunflowers. *Note:* Sunflowers seeds are choking hazards. Keep them out of your baby's and your toddler's reach during this family activity.

Baby

If your baby is around six months old, let him play with his own "pots" (nesting cups, small plastic bowls, or plastic cups) while his siblings plant. If you have other flowers in the yard, hold him close to them and show him how to sniff their aroma. If your baby is younger, set him in a bouncy seat near his siblings. He'll enjoy the smell of freshly dug soil and especially love watching water cascade from a watering can.

Toddler
While your older children plant the sunflower seeds, have your toddler practice planting. Give him a hand shovel and a pot, then let him fill it with soil. Show him how to pat down the soil to level it. He can then dig a small hole, plant a small rock, and pour water on it. If you like, fill a small watering can and ask your toddler to water any flowers in the yard.

Preschooler and School-Age Child
Your preschooler and school-age child can together plant sunflower seeds. Help them dig holes about half-inch deep and one foot apart, drop the seeds in the holes, then pat the soil down. These fast-growing seeds will require full sun exposure and a lot of water. Most sunflowers will grow to maturity within three to six months. Encourage your older children to monitor their sunflowers' growth. Perhaps they can record their observations in a journal or take photos of the sunflowers as they grow. During each visit (at least a few times a week), they can fill up a watering can and make sure the flowers have plenty of water.

Paws and Claws

Head out on a winter day with your children to look for animal tracks in the snow.

What You'll Need	All Ages	Baby	Toddler	Preschooler	School-Age Child
Warm clothes	🖐				
Regional guide to animal tracks	🖐				
Notebook and pencil					🖐

Make sure to dress your children warmly for this winter excursion. You also may want to wrap the baby in a fleece blanket. Before heading outdoors, talk to your children about the animals that visit your yard during the winter months. Tell them that each visiting animal leaves tracks, or prints, of its paws, feet, or hooves. Here are the tracks of animals common in many snowy parts of North America. You can find others in a regional guide to animal tracks.

Rabbit prints   Raccoon prints   Deer prints

Baby
Your baby will love the feeling of being bundled up cozy and warm while walking with her family out in the snow. When you come upon some tracks, crouch down and point them out to her. Even if she can't quite see the tracks, she'll love studying the snow as intently as her siblings do.

Toddler
In addition to scouting for animal tracks, ask your toddler about the tracks his family is making. Does he know which footprints belong to each family member? Challenge him to walk in a sibling's footprints.

Preschooler
Once your preschooler spots an animal track, encourage her to take a close look so she can describe it to her family. Ask her questions such as, "Is it a small or large track? Are there claw marks or other special patterns?" Your preschooler will appreciate her important detective role.

School-Age Child
Have your school-age child bring along a notebook and pencil to sketch the tracks. You and he can later compare the sketches to the illustrations on page 138 or to those in a regional animal guide. You may also want to check out websites such as www.bear-tracker.com for more information.

Won't Knock Us Down

This bottle game will be a knockout success!

What You'll Need	All Ages	Baby	Toddler	Preschooler	School-Age Child
Empty water bottles (with a bit of sand on the bottom to weigh them down)	🖐				
Foam balls	🖐				

Set up a number of bottles side by side in a line on a flat outdoor surface. Select one child to serve as a catcher who will stand behind the formation, retrieve the ball, and roll it back to the player. Everyone gets three tries each turn to roll a foam ball and knock down as many bottles as possible.

Baby

If your baby is crawling or walking with support, let her try to knock down the bottles. Set her in front of the bottles and let her make her way toward them. Cheer when she knocks a few down. If she needs motivation to aim for the bottles, let her watch her siblings take turns knocking them down with the ball. It won't take her long to figure out the game! If your baby isn't mobile yet, hold her in your lap near the bottles so she can reach out and swat them down. Guide her hands if she needs help.

Toddler

Your toddler can stand close to the bottles when it's her turn. She may be more apt to drop the ball into a roll, but try teaching her to set the ball on the ground then push it away from her.

Preschooler

Have your preschooler take three giant steps back from the bottles before he rolls the ball. After each turn, he should move three additional steps back. Encourage him to experiment with ways to line up and roll his ball accurately. Once he perfects his aim, can he even knock down bottles with his eyes closed?

School-Age Child

Chances are your school-age child will have more power than his other siblings. He will need to stand a good distance away when rolling. For an extra challenge, let his siblings space the bottles farther apart in the line. This way, the bottles will be less likely to strike one another and fall down like dominoes. He'll have to aim carefully at specific spots in the line to knock as many down as he can in three tries.

Water "Painting"

Unlike real painting projects, this water activity will never make a mess!

What You'll Need	All Ages	Baby	Toddler	Preschooler	School-Age Child
Buckets	✋				
Various paintbrushes	✋				
Chalk				✋	
Watch				✋	

On a warm day, send your children outside with a few buckets of water and clean paintbrushes. Let them "paint" the side of the house, the steps, the driveway, or their outdoor toys with the water. They'll enjoy giving the objects a nice sheen.

Baby

Brush your baby's feet with a bit of water. Creep the brush up his legs and then back down to his toes. He'll enjoy the sensation, especially if he's ticklish!

Toddler

Encourage your toddler to paint objects both high (like a wall) and low (like a driveway). Stretching and squatting will strengthen his major muscle groups. Give him a bigger paintbrush, which might be easier for him to handle.

Preschooler

Ask your preschooler to predict how much pavement she can paint in one minute. Mark her goal with chalk. Then challenge her to make that prediction come true. Keep track of the time on your watch, and cheer her on! See if she can paint an even bigger area next time.

School-Age Child

Have your school-age child write a secret, evaporating message with a paintbrush then invite you over to read it. Can you get there in time before it evaporates? You'll have to be quick! Encourage her to use different paintbrushes, different amounts of water, and different "canvases" to see how long she can make her message last. Write a message for her, too!

Watching the Clouds Pass By

Your children's imaginations will soar as they watch clouds.

What You'll Need	All Ages	Baby	Toddler	Preschooler	School-Age Child
Blanket	✋				
Cotton ball		✋			

Relax on a blanket with your children on a mostly sunny day and watch the clouds float by. Have your kids use their imaginations to describe the shapes and objects the clouds make. This activity is also great to do during a car ride. If your kids need distraction or entertainment, let the clouds help you!

Baby

Lay your baby on her back and point out the clouds to her. Show her how the clouds move by blowing gently on her face. She'll love the sensation. If you like, let your baby feel a "cloud" by rubbing a cotton ball on her hand or cheek.

Toddler

Depending on your toddler's vocabulary, he may suggest a cloud looks like a simple object, such as a circle, or a favorite object, such as a dog or truck. Have him lay on his back and try touching the cloud with his toes, elbows, hands, and even nose. This is a great way to have your busy toddler focus on the clouds for a little while!

Preschooler

Name a category such as animals, letters, or cars and ask your preschooler to point out clouds that look like something from that group. For instance, if you say "animal," she may see a cloud that looks like a dog.

School-Age Child

Your school-age child's ability to see detailed images in the clouds may amaze you. Let him tell a story about the things he sees in the sky, incorporating several cloud formations. As the clouds change and shift, his story will, too.

Parent Tip

Back inside, your children can re-create the clouds they saw using blue construction paper and cotton balls.

Did You Know?

In 1802, a scientist named Luke Howard classified clouds in three different groups: cumulus (puffy clouds), cirrus (wispy clouds), and stratus (clouds that blanket the sky).

Letterboxing

Letterboxing is a fun pastime that uses navigational skills to find hidden treasures in outdoor public places. Your children will love the hunt!

What You'll Need	All Ages	Baby	Toddler	Preschooler	School-Age Child
Stamp and ink pad (or carve a stamp from an eraser)	✋				
Notebook or journal and pen	✋				
Computer with Internet access and printer	✋				

Explain to your children that you'll be going on a search for a letterbox, a special container someone has hidden in your area. When you find it, you'll leave a stamp in its log book, plus make one in your family log book. Here are the steps to get started on your first letterbox hunt:

1. Think up a "trail name" with your children. This will be your family's letterboxing identity. You may want use your real name, but most letterboxers use a nickname or a name with special meaning.

2. Find a small rubber stamp and ink pad. Like your trail name, the stamp should represent something special about your family. You may wish to buy a special stamp beforehand or

make a homemade stamp by carving a special symbol into a large eraser.

3. Find a small notebook or blank journal to use as a family log book to record your finds. Don't forget to bring a pen, too.

4. Visit http://www.letterboxing.org to find lists of clues to letterboxes hidden in your area. According to the site, there are about twenty thousand letterboxes hidden in North America alone. Your older children may enjoy looking up clues with your supervision. When you've decided on a letterbox to find, print the clues.

5. Gather your gear and your team of hunters—it's time to head out! When at the site, encourage your children to follow the printed-out clues to find the letterbox. Remind them that letterboxing is an environmentally friendly activity; they should not dig, trample vegetation, or disturb wildlife during the hunt. When they've found the box, help them mark its log book with your stamp, write the name of your city, and date and sign it with your trail name. Remind your kids to record the find in the family log book using the stamp found in the letterbox.

Baby

Strap your baby into a carrier so he can feel like a participant on this hunt. Share the sense of adventure with him as you make your way to the hiding spot. With great animation, describe all the sights and sounds or sing silly parodies like, "Over the walkway and through the field, a-hunting we will go!"

Toddler

Your toddler will enjoy exploring with his family, especially if you end up in fun places like parks and playgrounds. Give him the special task of carrying the family stamp in his pocket. He can also be the one to stamp the log book found in the letterbox.

Preschooler

Once you find the letterbox, put your preschooler in charge of opening the family log book and marking it with the stamp from the letterbox. Ask him if he'd like you to add any additional notes to it about the search.

School-Age Child

Your school-age child should be the keeper of the clues. She can read each step out loud and offer instructions on which way to go next. She can also be in charge of recording your trail name, city, and the date next to your family stamp in the letterbox's log book. She can also add a few comments on the hiding space or the weather.

> I took my son and nephew on this adventure, and they loved it! It gave them a great sense of accomplishment when they found the letterbox.
>
> —Lisa

Raking 'Em Up

Turn the chore of raking leaves into a fun activity!

What You'll Need	All Ages	Baby	Toddler	Preschooler	School-Age Child
Rakes	🖐				
Blanket		🖐			
Stick				🖐	🖐

Head outside with your children on an autumn day. Rake some leaves into a pile and let your kids have fun in it!

Baby

Lay your baby on a blanket. Have her siblings show her a few vibrantly colored leaves and drop a few gently over her body. If your baby is six months or older, she can sit by a small pile of leaves and crunch them in her hands as you recite this poem:

Leaves orange, yellow, red.
"Crunch! Crunch!
Crunch! Crunch!"
That's what the leaves said.

Toddler

Jumping takes a lot of coordination. Help your toddler jump into the pile by holding her hands and jumping with her. You can also kneel in front of her, hold her under her arms, and lift her when she jumps.

Preschooler and School-Age Child

Preschoolers and school-age children have the body strength to rake. Have them work together to rake some leaves into a nice-size pile to test their jumping skills. Lay a stick about two feet from the pile. Have them stand behind the stick and try jumping into the pile of leaves. Did they reach the pile? Sing this song to give them the go-ahead to jump:

[Children's names] be nimble,
[children's names] run a mile,
[children's names] jump into the leaf pile!

If they hit the pile the first time, move the stick back another foot. Can they do it again?

Sprinkler Race

This sprinkler game will get your kids soaked and satisfied on a warm day!

What You'll Need	All Ages	Baby	Toddler	Preschooler	School-Age Child
Sprinkler	🖐				
Bucket			🖐	🖐	🖐
Plastic cups	🖐				
Watch			🖐	🖐	🖐

Set up a sprinkler and place a bucket a reasonable distance from it. Give your toddler, preschooler, and school-age child each a plastic cup and instruct them to use it to "collect" water from the sprinkler. The object of the game is to work as a team to transfer as much water as they can from their cups to the bucket within one minute. Depending on their strategy—and your sprinkler style—they can fill their cups simultaneously or do it as a relay. When one minute is up, tell them to stop and see how full the bucket is. Dump the water (use it to water the flowers or trees), then have them try to beat their amount.

Baby

As your older children run this race, hold your baby near the sprinkler's stream so she can feel the cool mist on her body and face. Fill a cup with water and let her dip her hands into it.

Toddler

Pouring the water into the bucket will be your toddler's favorite part, so he may not let his cup fill very long before running off to empty it. Let him enjoy the game in this way. Running back and forth is good for his legs, and pouring the water is good for his dexterity!

Preschooler

Challenge your preschooler to figure out how to get the most water in her cup in the shortest time. Where does she need to stand? How does she need to hold her cup? When she has a good strategy, have her share it with her teammates.

School-Age Child

Your school-age child will likely enjoy splashing around, but you can also use this activity to introduce math concepts like fractions and whole numbers. Ask him to predict how long it will take to fill the whole bucket. To do this, have him determine what fraction of the bucket they fill in one minute. Then help him use that fraction to predict how many more minutes it will take to fill the whole bucket. Have him inform the team that in the next round, they'll test his prediction.

Our Own Terrariums

Your children can collect some outdoor specimens in their own tiny terrariums.

hat You'll Need	All Ages	Baby	Toddler	Preschooler	School-Age Child
Plastic jars			🖐	🖐	🖐
Plastic water bottle		🖐			
Hand shovels	🖐				
Rocks, soil, leaves, and twigs	🖐				
Small toy animals or insects (or real bugs)	🖐				
Screwdriver or scissors				🖐	🖐

A terrarium is a container, usually enclosed, for observing and researching animals or plants. Your children can easily make their own play terrariums by each washing out a clear, deep plastic jar. When the jars are dry, go to your yard or a nearby park with your kids. Have them cover the bottom of their jars with rocks. Next, have them use a hand shovel to add a layer of soil over the rocks, then place leaves and twigs on top of the soil. Back home, give each child a small toy animal or insect to place on top of the leaves and twigs. Have them cover their jars and use their imaginations to note what's happening in the terrariums! Your older children may want real bugs instead (see next page).

Baby

Make a terrarium for your baby with an empty water bottle instead of a jar. Secure the top on the bottle. If your baby is six months or older, let her hold or even shake her terrarium. If she is younger, hold the bottle close to her so she can see what's inside.

Toddler

Help your toddler gather rocks and leaves for her terrarium. As you help her place them into her jar, count the number of leaves, rocks, and twigs out loud. Encourage her to count with you.

Preschooler and School-Age Child

Instead of adding plastic toys, your preschooler and school-age child may prefer to add live insects like caterpillars or ants to their terrariums. Make sure to punch air holes in the lids using a screwdriver or scissors, and have your children toss in a fresh leaf for food. Encourage them to handle the terrariums gently and note all they can about their insects before releasing them at the end of the activity.

Twig-and-Rock Houses

Build model homes with your children using twigs, rocks, or other natural materials.

What You'll Need	All Ages	Baby	Toddler	Preschooler	School-Age Child
Natural materials, such as rocks, twigs, and leaves	✋				

Head to your yard or nearby park with your children and help them collect twigs, rocks, or other natural materials. Have them sit in a flat, open space on grass or dirt, and then encourage them to use the materials to build houses. Your children can use their imaginations to construct the houses, or here are some building suggestions:

Rock House
Press long, flat rocks upright and side by side into the ground, and balance other rocks horizontally across the tops. Or simply make a rock pile in the shape of a house.

Twig House
Push similar-size twigs upright and side by side into the ground. Build four walls, then lay twigs horizontally across the top to create the roof.

Twig Tepee
Lean twigs upright against one another.

Baby

You and your baby can create a leaf "house." Put your baby in your lap as you pile leaves in a mound in front of you both. She may have just as much fun destroying her house as she does building it!

Toddler

To make her house, your toddler may enjoy simply lining up twigs and rocks or placing them on top of one another in a pile. For added fun, decorate her house's "yard" by arranging rocks and twigs to make the first letter of her name.

Preschooler and School-Age Child

Your preschooler and school-age child have experience with building blocks, but building with rocks and twigs will challenge them. Encourage them to combine some water and dirt to make mud that will better secure their building materials.

Up, Up, Paper Airplane

Help your children create and fly their own paper airplanes.

What You'll Need	All Ages	Baby	Toddler	Preschooler	School-Age Child
Construction paper			🖐	🖐	🖐
Small rocks				🖐	🖐
Marker				🖐	🖐
Sticks				🖐	🖐

Your children will love making paper airplanes as much as flying them. To make a basic paper airplane, follow these directions. You'll need to make an airplane for your toddler, but your older children should be able to make their own with a little help.

1. Place a sheet of construction paper in front of you so the short sides are horizontal and the long sides are vertical.
2. Fold down the top two corners to meet. This creates two triangle flaps.
3. Fold the paper in half so one triangle flap lies on the other. This will create a point.
4. Position the paper so the point faces to your left, the open edges are at the top, and the creased edge is at the bottom.
5. Fold down the top layer's edge to meet the bottom crease.
6. Flip the paper over so the triangle point faces to your right, then repeat step 5.

7. Pick up the paper from the long edge with one hand, and use the other hand to unfold the side flaps 90 degrees to create wings.

Baby

While your other children make and fly their paper airplanes, hold your baby and fly her like an airplane. If she is younger than four months, hold her face-up and use one hand to support her head and neck and the other hand to support her bottom. Gently sway her about six inches from your body. If she is older, you can hold her face-down, using one hand to support her chest and wrapping the other arm around her hips. If you like, sing the following song to the tune of "Mary Had a Little Lamb" as you fly your baby:

We are flying on a plane,
on a plane,
on a plane.
We are flying on a plane
way up here in the sky!

Toddler

Make a paper airplane for your toddler and show him how to fly it. He may need time to figure out how to release it properly. Regardless, applaud his efforts! If he becomes frustrated, encourage him to fly his airplane by holding it high while zooming around the yard.

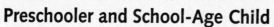

Preschooler and School-Age Child

Encourage your preschooler and school-age child to make their own paper airplanes. Help them when needed. They may need to make several practice airplanes before getting it right, so have several sheets of paper on hand. Here are some games they can play with their paper airplanes:

Aim Practice

Collect five small rocks and number them 1 through 5 with a marker. The numbers represent points. Place the rocks in random order a few feet from a starting point. Have your children stand at the starting point and fly their airplanes toward the rocks. When they land, note the rock each is nearest. The number on the respective rock is the number of points that child earns. Continue to play until one child earns ten points.

Plane Landing

Use two sticks to create a start and finish line a few feet apart. Have your children fly their airplanes from the start line toward the finish line. Wherever they land, your children must collect them and throw them again from that spot. Have them continue until one of them flies a plane across the finish line.

Up and Away

Have your children fly their airplanes into the air and count how long they each stay afloat. Whose flies the longest?

Beanbag Race

Use homemade beanbags to run this fun race.

What You'll Need	All Ages	Baby	Toddler	Preschooler	School-Age Child
Large socks of different colors	🖐				
Dried beans	🖐				
Rubber bands	🖐				
Long and short sticks	🖐				

Help your children fill large socks with dried beans. Try to give each child a sock of a different color from the others. Tightly close the socks with rubber bands. Then head outside to a fairly flat grassy area with the beanbags. Make a start line with a long stick and have your kids stand behind it. On the count of three, have your children toss their beanbags as far as they can in front of them. After the bags have landed, have your children race to collect them and return to the start line. The first child to cross the start line wins. Race again as often as your kids want. If they like, have them forgo the race and just have fun with the beanbags as described below.

Baby

A beanbag will delight your baby's senses. Rub the sock up and down his body and along his cheek, letting the beans massage him. If he can grasp objects, give him the beanbag and let him strengthen his finger muscles as he feels the beans. If your baby is beginning to show signs of standing and walking, he can "run" the beanbag race, too! Help him toss his beanbag, then support him under his arms while he tries to walk and collect it.

Toddler
Because your toddler is learning to hold and release objects, it may be easier for her to toss her beanbag upward than forward. Encourage her to throw it as many times as needed to get it to a designated spot a short distance from the start line.

Preschooler
Tossing beanbags will strengthen your preschooler's large motor skills. Encourage him to throw his beanbag overhand, underhand, and backward over his shoulder. Can he think of other ways to toss it? Which way tosses the bag the farthest?

School-Age Child
Your school-age child can track her beanbag tosses by marking where each attempt lands with a short stick. Encourage her to beat her best toss. For a more physical challenge, tell her to hop to retrieve her beanbag and skip back to the start line. Her siblings may try to mimic her actions.

Hop with Me

This classic sidewalk game is sure to get the whole family hopping!

What You'll Need	All Ages	Baby	Toddler	Preschooler	School-Age Child
Chalk	✋				
Small rock	✋				
Beanbag (see page 160 for a homemade variety)			✋		

On a sidewalk or driveway, help your older children draw a chalk hopscotch court with ten connecting boxes like so:

1. Begin by drawing Box 1.
2. Draw two boxes side by side centered over Box 1, and number them 2 and 3.
3. Move up and draw Box 4 centered over Boxes 2 and 3.
4. Draw Boxes 5 and 6 side by side centered over Box 4.
5. Move up and draw Box 7 centered over Boxes 5 and 6.
6. Draw Boxes 8 and 9 side by side centered over Box 7.
7. Lastly, move up and draw Box 10 centered over Boxes 8 and 9.

Teach your children how to play traditional hopscotch: For a player's first turn, she must toss a small rock onto the first square on the court, and then hop through the court without landing on the first square. When landing on the single boxes, the player must hop on one foot. When landing on the side-by-side boxes, she must straddle the boxes with one foot on each. On the way back through the court, she must stop and pick up the rock before continuing on. On her second turn, she must toss the rock on the second square, and so on with each round. If her rock misses a box, if she loses her balance, or if she steps on a line, her turn is over. With her next turn, she picks up where she left off.

Encourage your children to play the traditional form of hopscotch or the following age-appropriate variations:

Baby

If your baby is around six months old, hold her up so she can "walk" her way through the hopscotch court. If you like, bounce slightly as you move along. If she is younger than six months, hold her in your arms and gently bounce along the hopscotch court. She'll love the fun movement.

Toddler

Hold your toddler's hand and walk through the hopscotch court as you count the number in each square out loud. Instead of a rock, give her a beanbag to toss onto the court (so there's less danger if she loses control of her aim), and see if she can name the number it lands on. Have her retrieve the bag and toss it again. If she likes, let her bounce or hop through court however she wishes.

Preschooler

At this age, preschoolers may not have mastered hopping on one foot, so challenge your preschooler to give it a try through the hopscotch court. If he has trouble hopping the entire court on one foot, let him jump with two feet through the court.

School-Age Child

Once your school-age child has mastered the traditional hopscotch court, have her try another version called Snail. In this variation, draw the court to look like a snail shell (see right). Have her choose one foot to hop on to reach the center. She can hop only once in each square and can't hop on any lines. If she hops in a square more than once or hops on any lines, she'll have to start over.

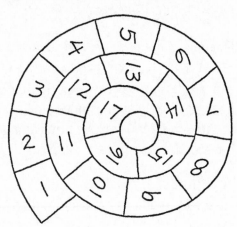

CHAPTER 5
Out & About

Ah, the car ride: the whining kids, the bathroom emergencies, the two-minute errands that end up taking two hours...
                                                            —Heather

We know you've got places to go—and we know you have to take your kids with you. But who says you all can't enjoy the ride? This chapter holds true to the belief that life happens during the journey. Here you'll find simple, creative ideas to have fun while out and about, such as when you're riding in a car, sitting in a restaurant, or waiting in a checkout line. And because you're on the go, most of these activities require only your imaginations!

Freeze!

Here's a fun, easy way to entertain your children while in the car, a waiting room, or anywhere else that requires patience.

What You'll Need	All Ages	Baby	Toddler	Preschooler	School-Age Child
Your hands and some imagination!	✋				

To begin the game, start clapping a steady rhythm. (If your hands aren't free, say "chug, chug" in rhythm while your children clap.) Ask your children to join in. After a moment or so, say, "Freeze!" and stay completely still and quiet. Your children will follow the command, but they'll eventually start giggling! Have your children take turns leading the clapping and saying, "Freeze!" If you're someplace where clapping isn't appropriate (for example, in a quiet waiting room), do a silent action, like patting your belly or making a goofy face.

Baby

If your baby is six months or older, he may join in with his siblings as they clap. Encourage your older children to praise him for his efforts! If your baby is younger, you or his siblings can gently help him clap his hands until someone says, "Freeze!" He'll love the rhythm and movement.

Toddler

Your toddler will enjoy anticipating the command to freeze, but she may have trouble following it. To help her focus on the command, use a nearby object as a visual cue. This object can be a crayon, toy, sippy cup, or other handy object (including your own hand). Tell her that when the leader says, "Freeze!" and holds up the object, she must stay still until the object is lowered.

Preschooler

Many preschoolers love to be goofy. When it's your preschooler's turn to lead the clapping, have her make silly noises to accompany her actions. If noise isn't appropriate where you are, suggest that she make a silly face instead. When it's time to freeze, regaining her composure may be a challenge, so encourage her efforts.

School-Age Child

Along with clapping, your school-age child may want to challenge his siblings with other actions. For example, he may put his hands on his knees or touch his nose between each clap. When he gives the command to freeze, he may challenge his siblings to not just stay still, but to also close their eyes or fold their hands.

> My eight-month-old son learned to clap during one of these games. He loved copying the movements of his older brother.
>
> —Lisa

Table Memory

While waiting at a restaurant, keep your kids busy with this fun memory game.

What You'll Need	All Ages	Baby	Toddler	Preschooler	School-Age Child
Items on the restaurant table	✋				

While sitting at a restaurant table, place three different items in front of you. Ask your children to identify them, then have them close their eyes. Move one item to your lap. Have them open their eyes and tell you which item is missing. Your children can then take turns hiding an item and challenging the other siblings' memories.

Baby

Your baby may be too young to play this memory game, but he can play another type of memory game: peekaboo! Peekaboo strengthens his sense of object permanence (the understanding that something exists even when not in sight). Encourage your older children to play peekaboo with your baby using a napkin, the menu, or other item.

Toddler

After you hide an item in your lap, your toddler may not be as quick as his older siblings to identify it. To give him a chance to test his memory, encourage your older kids to let him identify the missing item at least once. When it's your toddler's turn to hide an item, have your older kids close their eyes while you prompt him to hide an item in his lap.

Preschooler

To further challenge your preschooler's memory, rearrange the order of the items after hiding one. After she correctly identifies the missing item, ask her put the other items in their original order. When it's your preschooler's turn to hide an item, encourage her to give her siblings a hint that describes the missing item. For example, she may say, "I took away something red."

School-Age Child

Challenge your school-age child to pay close attention to detail. After she correctly identifies a missing item, ask her a more detailed question about it, such as, "What color is the label on the ketchup bottle?" or "What kind of jelly is in the packet?"

These Little Kids Went to the Market

Here's a fun way to make grocery shopping a team effort!

What You'll Need	All Ages	Baby	Toddler	Preschooler	School-Age Child
Supermarket flyers or magazines	🖐				
Child-safe scissors	🖐				
Index cards	🖐				
Glue sticks	🖐				
Crayons	🖐				

Before your next trip to the supermarket, tell your older children a few items from your grocery list. They can cut out pictures of those items from supermarket flyers or magazines, then glue the pictures onto separate index cards. Or they can draw pictures of the items with crayons. When it's time to go to the supermarket, give your toddler, preschooler, and school-age child each a few cards and ask them, "What's the food on your card?" After they've identified the item, say, "Your job is to look for this food as we shop. Will you help me do that?"

Baby

The grocery store is full of educational opportunities for your baby. Encourage her siblings to show her the items they find from their cards and describe them to her. For example, "This is a red, crunchy apple." Your baby will enjoy the colors, smells, and interaction.

Toddler

When you get close to an item on your toddler's card, prompt him by saying, "Do you see the yellow bananas? They are very close now." When he identifies the item, let him hold it and examine it. Talk to him about each item, such as, "These bananas are smooth and yellow." This will support his growing vocabulary.

Preschooler and School-Age Child

In addition to creating cards for everyday items on your grocery list, your preschooler and school-age child may enjoy making cards for ingredients in a favorite dish or meal. For example, tell them that this week you will make tacos. Ask them to help you determine what items you need to buy for the meal, and have them create cards for those items. At the store, give them the cards so they can collect the ingredients for this special meal.

Parent Tip
Create cards of items you buy often (for example, bread, eggs, milk, bananas, and so on) and use them every time you visit the supermarket with your children.

Diddle, Diddle, Doo

While riding in the car with your children, recite this knee-slapping, silly rhyme that talks about important people in your community.

What You'll Need	All Ages	Baby	Toddler	Preschooler	School-Age Child
Hands and knees!	✋				

As you teach your kids the rhyme, show them how to slap each hand on each knee at the same time in rhythm. (If you're driving, wait until a stoplight so your hands are free to demonstrate the slaps.) Once they have the rhythm down, lead them with this rhyme:

Hey, diddle, diddle,
who's in the middle
when you're feeling sick?
A doctor, that's who!
Diddle, diddle, doo.
GO DOCTOR!

Hey, diddle, diddle,
who's in the middle
when there is a fire?
A firefighter, that's who!
Diddle, diddle, doo.
GO FIREFIGHTER!

Hey, diddle, diddle,
who's in the middle
when you need the mail?
A mailman, that's who!
Diddle, diddle, doo.
GO MAILMAN!

Hey, diddle, diddle,
who's in the middle
when you want to learn?
A teacher, that's who!
Diddle, diddle, doo.
GO TEACHER!

Baby and Toddler

Your baby and toddler will enjoy listening to everyone recite this rhyme and slap knees. They may even try to slap their own knees! If you like, help your toddler make the connection between the people described in the rhyme and the people he knows. For example, after reciting the verse about the doctor, say to your toddler, "A doctor is someone who makes you feel all better. Dr. Jones is your doctor. You know who she is, don't you?"

Preschooler and School-Age Child

Encourage your preschooler and school-age child to come up with more people in the community to add to the rhyme, like a police officer, librarian, or garbage collector. When finished reciting the rhyme, ask your children what they think of each person's job. Does it sound fun, easy, or hard? This exercise may get them thinking about what they want to be when they grow up.

> This activity is my family's favorite during car trips.
> —Lisa

Where Is Everyone Going?

With imagination and storytelling, family car rides are entertaining! During your next family car ride, let your older children take turns telling a tale about the people in a nearby car.

What You'll Need	All Ages	Baby	Toddler	Preschooler	School-Age Child
Imagination!	✋				

Baby

Although your baby is too young to tell a story, she will enjoy listening to one told by a loved one. She may even coo and smile as a way to interact with her sibling when she hears his happy voice and sees his smile as he tells the story. Her siblings can nurture her own "storytelling" skills by responding to her babbles with questions such as, "And then what happened?"

Toddler

As your toddler listens to the tale, he may join in when he hears a word he recognizes. For instance, if the storyteller says, "That man in the car looks like Papa," your toddler may look to see for himself and yell, "Papa!" Let him get involved in this way—it shows his listening skills are developing! If you like, have your older children further involve him in the storytelling by asking him questions such as "Where is that car going?"

Preschooler and School-Age Child

To help your preschooler and school-age child begin their stories, ask a few leading questions, such as "Who do you think is in the car ahead of us? Where do you think they're going? What are they going to do there?" Encourage your children to use their imaginations to answer these questions and spin a tale! Your school-age child may not need these questions to start her story; in that case, say simply, "Tell me about the people traveling behind us."

> I love doing this activity with my children. My pre-schooler inevitably drops a hint about where he wishes he were headed. For example, he'll say, "I think that man is going to the ice-cream store because he is SO hungry for ice cream!"
>
> —Heather

ABC Games

These alphabet games are fun ways to pass time while waiting with your children in a doctor's office, in a checkout line, or another place that requires patience.

What You'll Need	All Ages	Baby	Toddler	Preschooler	School-Age Child
Scrap paper and pencil				🖐	

Baby

Use your baby's first name in a cheer with his siblings. Your baby will love to hear his family cheer for him! For example:

You: "Give me an *A*!"
Children: "*A*!"
You: "Give me a *D*!"
Children: "*D*!"
You: "Give me an *A*!"
Children: "*A*!"
You: "Give me an *M*!"
Children: "*M*!"
You: "What's that spell?"
Children: "ADAM!"

Toddler

Show your toddler a highly visible, large letter, such as one in a magazine title. Say the letter several times, then ask her to repeat it. To use her sense of touch to help remember the formation of the letter, have her trace the letter with her finger. If she can't reach the letter, use your finger to draw it on the back of her hand.

Preschooler

If your preschooler knows how to spell his name, challenge him to find each letter somewhere around him. Then encourage him to find the letters in other words he knows how to spell. If your preschooler doesn't know how to spell his name or another word, print the word on scrap paper and have him find each letter around him.

School-Age Child

Have your school-age child locate each letter of the alphabet somewhere around her. She must find each letter in order, which means she must find an *A* before finding a *B* and so on. She may need to say, "Pass" for hard-to-find letters. If you like, keep track of the time it takes her to find the letters and have her repeat the activity to see whether she can beat that time.

Ten Things

This fun counting game will keep your children's attention when you're out and about.

What You'll Need	All Ages	Baby	Toddler	Preschooler	School-Age Child
Scrap paper and pen				🖐	🖐

To play, pose a question to your children that requires ten answers. For example, point to a car ahead of you and say, "I wonder what that family likes to eat for dinner. Can we come up with ten things you think they like to eat?" Here are other ideas for questions:

- "Can you name ten things that truck driver may have in his truck?"
- "Can you name ten kinds of fruit?"
- "Can you name ten things the baby does before he goes to bed?"
- "Can you name ten things you may find in the kitchen of a restaurant?"

Baby

Your baby can't contribute answers, but he can still participate. For example, he will love to hear his siblings recite the following number rhyme that counts from one to ten:

How much do we love baby?
We love baby—one.
We love baby—one,
because he's so much fun!
How much do we love baby?
We love baby—two.
We love baby—two,
because he loves us, too!

To continue, ask your other children to make up rhyming responses for the remaining numbers up to ten.

Toddler
You can involve your toddler in the activity by asking a question specific to her. For example, if the question is "What are ten things [toddler's name] likes to eat," ask your toddler, "Do you like to eat bananas?" If she says yes, then she's contributed bananas to the list.

Preschooler and School-Age Child
Your older children can likely provide ten answers to every question. To keep track, they can make a mark on a scrap of paper for every answer they give. Make sure they count the toddler's contributions, too! You can also customize the questions to fit their specific interests. For example, if your preschooler loves dinosaurs, ask him to name ten facts about dinosaurs. If your school-age child is currently studying geography at school, ask her to name ten states.

What Do You Hear?

This fun game will have your kids sounding like the animals, cars, and other things around them!

What You'll Need	All Ages	Baby	Toddler	Preschooler	School-Age Child
Voices!	🖐				

When you and your children are out on a walk, in the car, or in a restaurant, ask them to be quiet for a moment to listen to the sounds around them. What do they hear? Then have each child take a turn using only her voice to imitate something she hears. Everyone else tries to guess the source of the sound she's imitating.

Baby

Your baby will enjoy listening to her siblings play this game, but she may want to make some noise herself. If she coos or happily emits a high-pitched squeal, say to your other children, "Your baby sister wants to share, too! What does that sound remind you of?"

Toddler

By this age, your toddler may know how to make many sounds with his voice, but he may need some direction to play this game. When it's his turn to imitate a sound, privately discuss with him a sound you've heard in the area. For example, ask him, "Can you hear the big trucks driving by? What sound do they make?" Otherwise, prompt him to make a particular sound for his turn. For example, say, "What does a cow say?"

Preschooler and School-Age Child

Your preschooler and school-age child can take separate turns, or for a special challenge, you can encourage them to work together to create a "soundscape" of multiple sources. Have them listen and look around the area for ideas, whisper their plans to each other, then perform the sounds. For instance, if they decide to imitate a dog and its owner, one can bark and the other can say a command like "Heel!"

CHAPTER 6
Learning & Exploring

Kids learn best from one another. At an early age, I loved learning so much, I recruited neighborhood children to come to my basement for math and art lessons. I had a chalkboard, makeshift desks, and even, for an unlucky few, some homework!
—Lisa

This chapter proves nearly anything can be an educational experience for children. Whether these activities cultivate a love of reading and writing, inspire the art of storytelling, or experiment with simple science, they'll have your kids learning and exploring together. In each one, we provide ideas for creating a "classroom" with simple materials and instructions to challenge and engage your children's minds.

Spin the Storybox

Design simple, reusable storyboxes to spark your children's storytelling skills.

What You'll Need	All Ages	Baby	Toddler	Preschooler	School-Age Child
Old picture books and magazines	✋				
Empty cube-shaped tissue box	✋				
Child-safe scissors and glue	✋				
Index card	✋				
Journal or notebook and pencil					✋

Have your children search through magazines to find pictures of animals, people, toys, and other objects that strike their fancy. Decide as a family which six images to cut out. Then create a storybox by gluing one picture onto each side of a cube-shaped tissue box. Before gluing a picture to the top of the box, cut and glue an index card to cover the dispensing hole. When the storybox is complete, have your children take turns being the storyteller, who tosses or rolls the storybox to see which picture lands face-up. The storyteller must then tell a story to his siblings about the image. Encourage the storytellers to let their imaginations run free when telling the tales.

Baby

Your baby can't tell much of a tale, but she will love snuggling with you as she watches the colorful storybox and listens to her siblings spin stories. When it's your baby's turn to be the storyteller, you can make up a tale from her perspective.

Toddler

When it's your toddler's turn to be the storyteller, encourage him to identify the picture and talk a little about it. This exercise will strengthen his fledgling vocabulary and language skills.

For example, you may say, "This is a clock. Can you say 'clock'?" Whatever response he gives, say, "Yeah! That's right, 'clock'!" Then help him create a sentence with the word in it: "The clock says it's noon, and the kids have to come inside for lunch."

Preschooler

Your preschooler's growing imagination will let her tell an entertaining story. Encourage her to weave parts of her everyday life into her tale. For example, she may include her siblings, friends, or preschool. This activity may even give you insight into your preschooler's thoughts or feelings about situations in her daily life. (See below.)

School-Age Child

Challenge your school-age child to include the elements of a formal story when telling his tale. He can make sure his story has a setting, different characters, a conflict, a solution, and a closing. After the activity, encourage him to record and perhaps continue his stories in a journal or notebook.

> Through this activity, I learned about something that had happened at my son's preschool—feelings he was still trying to sort out. My three-year-old used a picture on his storybox to describe two boys fighting over a toy and a teacher taking the toy away.
>
> —Lisa

Bark Rubbings

Take your children outside to make rubbings of the bark on trees in your yard or neighborhood park.

What You'll Need	All Ages	Baby	Toddler	Preschooler	School-Age Child
Paper			🖐	🖐	🖐
Jumbo crayons with wrappers removed			🖐	🖐	🖐
Duct tape			🖐	🖐	🖐
Glue sticks			🖐	🖐	🖐
Stapler			🖐	🖐	🖐
Tree guide			🖐	🖐	🖐
Blanket		🖐			
Pen				🖐	🖐

Before heading out to the yard or the park, give your toddler, preschooler, and school-age child each a bare jumbo crayon and a sheet of paper. Once outside, have your children select their trees—each a different kind, if possible. Attach each child's paper to the tree with duct tape. Instruct your children to firmly rub the length of the crayon up and down the paper to make bark rubbings. Before heading back home, have them each pick up a leaf that's fallen from their respective trees.

When back inside, help your children glue their leaves onto the paper with their bark rubbings. When done, stack the papers and staple them together along the left side to create a tree book. Together, identify the trees in your book and label each page with the appropriate tree name. If you like, look through a guide on the trees in your area to learn more.

Baby

While your older children do this activity, you can delight your baby's senses with the tree. Rub her palm gently on its bark and the leaves. She'll enjoy the different textures. Then lay her on a blanket under the tree so she can watch the leaves fluttering in the wind.

Toddler

Your toddler may need assistance when making her rubbing, since she's still developing her ability to hold and manipulate objects such as crayons. Rubbing a tree with a rough surface may make it even more challenging. Guide her hands to help her gently move her crayon up and down on the paper. She may want to fill only a small portion of the paper with the rubbing. Back inside, she can add a leaf rubbing, too. Set a leaf on the table, lay her paper over it, and tape it in place. She'll enjoy making the leaf outline appear!

Preschooler

Your preschooler's vocabulary is growing incredibly, especially with descriptive words. When you're home, encourage him to describe his tree to you. Record his description on his paper.

School-Age Child

Back home, encourage your school-age child to write a story or a poem on his paper about the many wonderful things trees provide, like shade, fruit, nuts, shelters for animals, and more.

Sticking to Our ABCs

Use alphabet magnets to reinforce letter learning in your home.

What You'll Need	All Ages	Baby	Toddler	Preschooler	School-Age Child
Metal baking sheets (or pans)	✋				
Alphabet magnets	✋				

Give each child a metal baking sheet, then spread out a set of alphabet magnets so all your children can reach it. No matter what their ages, the children will have fun moving, sorting, and arranging the letters.

Baby

It's never too early to introduce letters to your baby. If he's six months or older, place him in his highchair and let him have fun pushing the letters around a baking sheet. He'll enjoy pulling each letter off and putting it back on the sheet. If he's younger than six months, arrange the letters to spell his name on the sheet. Say each letter out loud as you place it on the sheet. Even though he won't recognize his name, the contrast of the colored letters against the shiny metal will attract his attention.

Toddler

Your toddler will use this activity to practice her sorting and arranging skills more than her letter recognition. Your toddler may work hard to arrange the letters on her baking sheet, only to take them off and create a new arrangement on the table. Before she creates a new arrangement, point to and name each letter for her.

Preschooler

At this age, your preschooler may be discovering that letters come together to form words, including his own name. He may even make up words with the magnets and ask you what they spell. Play along and sound out his creations as best you can. This exercise is a wonderful way to build the foundation for reading.

School-Age Child

Your school-age child can read and spell, so give her a special challenge with the alphabet magnets. Help her create a long word at the top of her baking sheet, like *family* or *holiday*. Then ask her how many other words she can create by using just those letters.

Parent Tip

If you don't have alphabet magnets, you and your older children can create a homemade set. Cut out large letters from magazines, then glue the letters onto small square pieces of cardboard cut out from a cereal box. Finally, stick a magnetic strip to the back of each piece.

Opposite Olympics

Room by room, you and your children can explore opposites.

What You'll Need	All Ages	Baby	Toddler	Preschooler	School-Age Child
Notebook and pencil					✋

As a family, take a tour of your home and seek out opposites. Turn lights on and off. Fill a bucket with toys, then empty it. Go up a step, then down one. Make a happy face, then a sad one. Hold a piece of ice, then touch warm water. Hug a soft teddy bear, then touch the hard floor. Explain to your children that these objects, actions, and feelings are opposites.

Baby

Your baby will love taking this tour with his siblings. If he's at least six months old, perhaps he can flick the light switch on and off, or take part in emptying the toy bins and filling them up. Be sure to emphasize the opposite words as he does the actions: "The light is *on*. The light is *off*." This is an important time for him as he builds his vocabulary and links words to objects and effects. If your baby is younger, he'll enjoy playing this simple opposites game: Wave and say "goodbye" to him as you walk away, then quickly return and wave and say "hello." He'll love the repetition and may want you to do it again and again.

Toddler

During the house tour, don't be surprised if your toddler becomes particularly enthralled with one activity (for example, turning on and off the lights). In addition to learning about opposites, he's learning about cause and effect, thinking, "I flip this switch, and a light goes on. I flip it again, and then it goes off." This activity helps him learn how his actions create a result.

Preschooler

Your preschooler can likely name the opposites of things she discovers during the tour. To encourage her, say, "We are going up the step. What is the opposite of up?" or "This water is cold. What's the opposite of cold?" Chances are, you will be surprised by all the opposites she knows.

School-Age Child

Your school-age child can keep track of the opposites her family discovers on the tour. Give her a notebook and a pencil, and have her write each pair of opposites ("up/down" or "on/off") as you come across them. Or she can go ahead of her family and identify opposites in the next room. When her siblings arrive, she may say, "I found five opposites in here. Can you find them?" Encourage her to give hints when necessary.

Parent Tip
This activity can be a fun, clever way to remind your children of manners or tidiness. For example, you may say, "This living room needs to be the opposite of messy!"

All About Us

Your children will learn about themselves and one another with this fun activity!

What You'll Need	All Ages	Baby	Toddler	Preschooler	School-Age Child
Light-colored construction paper	🖐				
Marker	🖐				
Crayons and stickers	🖐				
Paper clips	🖐				
Yarn	🖐				
Tape	🖐				
Tape measure	🖐				
Bathroom scale	🖐				

For each child, use a marker to write the following list down the left side of a separate sheet of light-colored construction paper. Your school-age child can help with this task.

Name *Eye color*
Birthday *Favorite color*
Height *Favorite food*
Weight *Favorite book*
Hair color *Hobbies*

See below for ways to help your children write responses to the list on their sheets. Then let them decorate their sheets with crayons or stickers. When the sheets are finished, use paper clips to secure them to a 5-foot piece of yarn to make a banner. Use tape to prominently display the banner in your home.

Baby

Have your other children help you come up with your baby's responses. For example, they may suggest that eating or napping are her hobbies. To determine her favorite color, they can hold up toys in different colors and see which one gets the best reaction from her.

Toddler

Your toddler may need help expressing his responses, which you can then write down. For example, when determining his favorite color, you may say, "Do you like red? Our couch is red. Or do you like blue? Your shirt is blue." You can also determine his favorite book by pointing to a few books you've read together and letting him decide which is his favorite.

Preschooler

Help your preschooler by recording her responses on her sheet. If she's learning to write, challenge her to write her name in the appropriate spot. For extra help, print her name on another sheet of paper and have her copy the letters on her sheet. When she's done, encourage her to draw a picture of herself on her sheet. She can draw herself doing one of her hobbies or enjoying one of her favorite things.

School-Age Child

At the beginning of the activity, your school-age child can help you measure and weigh his siblings. For a fun exercise, have him estimate the height and weight of each sibling (including himself) before taking the measurements.

Parent Tip

When you're done displaying the banner, be sure to store it in a safe place. It's a great keepsake for years to come, and your children may enjoy looking at it as they grow.

Weather Watch

Track the local weather with these simple weather cards.

What You'll Need	All Ages	Baby	Toddler	Preschooler	School-Age Child
Index cards	✋				
Crayons	✋				
Poster board	✋				
Sticky Back Velcro	✋				
Tape	✋				
Weather thermometer				✋	
Weather resources, such as newspapers or almanacs					✋

As a family, discuss the weather conditions you experience in your area throughout the year (sunny, cloudy, windy, rainy, snowy, and so on). Have your preschooler and school-age child draw a picture on separate index cards for each of these weather conditions. Then write "Today's Weather" at the top of a large sheet of poster board. Cut Sticky Back Velcro strips, and affix a loop half to the back of each card. Affix two or three (or more) hook halves to the construction paper.

When you're done, have the kids look out a window or go outside to identify your current weather. Have them stick the appropriate card(s) to the board. Keep these weather cards by a window, and each morning ask your kids to display the cards that describe that day's weather. Below are some additional ways each child can enjoy the weather board.

Baby

Each day while your older children observe the weather, use the opportunity to teach your baby words that describe the weather. For example, say, "Your brothers are looking at the leaves blowing around on the ground. That means it's *windy*." If you like, further illustrate the weather by gently blowing on his face to imitate wind. Take your baby to the window (or outside if properly dressed) to experience the weather as you describe it.

Toddler

In addition to seeing the weather through a window, your toddler can feel the weather. For example, open a window or door and have him reach his hand outside. Ask him, "How does that feel? Cold? Wet? Windy?" The tactile exercise will help him connect words with their meanings.

Preschooler

Preschoolers love to make their own decisions, so after determining the day's weather, have him decide what type of clothing he should wear. Should he wear a hat and scarf or sandals and shorts? Your preschooler may also want to know the temperature before choosing his clothing, so display a thermometer outside a window. Use simple terms to explain how to read it. If it's a mercury thermometer, say, "The shorter the red line is, the colder it is outside. And the longer the red line is, the warmer it is."

School-Age Child

Before bedtime each night, challenge your school-age child to forecast the next day's weather. She may choose to watch a weather segment on the evening news; read the weather section in the daily paper; visit a weather website (with your supervision); or read a book about weather predictions, like *The Old Farmer's Almanac for Kids*. She can then see whether her predictions are right!

Number Match Up

All your kids will enjoy playing with these homemade number cards.

What You'll Need	All Ages	Baby	Toddler	Preschooler	School-Age Child
20 index cards	✋				
Crayons	✋				
Small stickers	✋				

Help your children create two sets of ten index cards. On one set, number the cards 1 through 10 (one number per card). On the other set, place one sticker on the first card, two stickers on the second card, three stickers on the third card, and so on until you place ten stickers on the tenth card. Once they're finished, your children can play the following age-appropriate games with the cards.

Baby

Teach your other children to recite the following rhyme to your baby. Each time they say a number, they can hold up both its numeral and sticker cards. She'll enjoy watching the cards and listening to her siblings.

One, two—we love you.
Three, four—we'll teach you more.
Five, six—[your baby's name] we pick.

Seven, eight—arms out straight.
Nine, ten—we hug again!

Toddler

Help your toddler begin to recognize numbers using the cards.
Place a sticker card in front of him and ask, "How many stickers do you see here?" Count out loud together as you point to
each sticker. Say, "One, two—I see two stickers." Then show
him the corresponding numeral card and say, "This is the
number 2."

Preschooler

Your preschooler can play a memory game with the cards.
Show her how to shuffle the two sets of cards together, then
lay them face-down in five rows of four cards. Have her turn
over one card, then turn over another card. If she matches a
sticker card to its corresponding numeral card, she keeps
both. If they don't match, she turns them back over. See how
many turns she takes to match all the pairs.

School-Age Child

Here's a fun, challenging math game for your school-age
child: Have him randomly pick a sticker card. Tell him that
number is the "answer" to a math problem—one he must
create with the numeral cards! For instance, if he drew the
card with 7 stickers, he could then pick up the 3 and 4
numeral cards because 3 plus 4 equals 7.

Window Painting

Let your children practice writing in an unusual way—by painting on a window!

What You'll Need	All Ages	Baby	Toddler	Preschooler	School-Age Child
Newspaper, tape, and large sheet	🖐				
Old T-shirts or smocks	🖐				
Window paint (1 part powdered tempera paint and 1 part clear liquid dishwasher detergent)	🖐				
Shallow bowls	🖐				
Paintbrushes	🖐				

Choose a large glass window or door in your home that all your kids can easily reach. The paint will wash off glass, but tape newspaper to the wall below the glass and spread a large sheet on the floor. Have your children put on old T-shirts or smocks to protect their clothes. Then mix different-colored batches of window paint and pour the paint into shallow bowls. Give your kids each a paintbrush and a bowl, assign them a section of glass, and let them start painting!

Baby

If your baby is six months or older, let her hold a small paintbrush as you help her write a letter or draw a line. If you like,

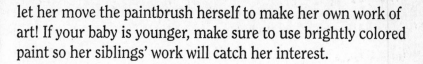

let her move the paintbrush herself to make her own work of art! If your baby is younger, make sure to use brightly colored paint so her siblings' work will catch her interest.

Toddler
Your toddler will love to make her mark on the glass! Show her how to dip the paintbrush in the paint, then brush it lightly on the glass. Hold her hand and help her write the first letter of her name on the window. Mention the shapes and lines found in that letter and say them as you paint together. *"B is for Brooke. Let's draw a straight line and then two half circles to make a B."*

Preschooler
If possible, assign your preschooler to a window or door with a lattice. Challenge him to spell his name or another simple word one letter per pane. If you don't have a lattice, draw one on the glass for him to use. If necessary, spell the word for him letter by letter as he writes.

School-Age Child
Have your school-age child practice writing in different sizes. For example, he can write very small letters with a small paintbrush and very large letters with a large paintbrush. If he's learning how to write in cursive, this activity is a fun, artistic way to practice!

What Floats?

In this activity, your children will discover what items float and what ones sink.

What You'll Need	All Ages	Baby	Toddler	Preschooler	School-Age Child
Immersible objects, including a small ball, rock, bottle cap, apple or orange, Ping-Pong ball, cotton ball, metal fork, wooden block, bath toys, marbles, and so on	🖐				
Large clear bowl	🖐				
Small bowl		🖐			
Clear plastic bottle		🖐			

To begin, gather a variety of small immersible objects from around the home. Then fill a large clear bowl with water and have your children gather around it. Ask them whether they think each item will float or sink. Take turns testing each item by dropping it into the bowl.

Baby

While he watches your older children discover what objects sink or float, your baby can experiment with water, too. If your baby is six months or older, put him in his highchair, then set a small bowl of water in front of him. Place a Ping-Pong ball (or other floatable ball) in the water, and encourage him to reach for it. If your baby is younger, fill a clear plastic bottle with water, drop in a marble, then secure the bottle closed. Shake it gently in front of him so he can track the marble as it rolls back and forth.

Toddler

Show your toddler what *floating* means to help her understand the purpose of the activity. First put a light object, like a Ping-Pong ball, in the bowl. Then say, "See the ball on top of the water? It's floating." Then remove the light item and drop a heavy object, like a rock, into the water. Say, "See the rock on the bottom of the bowl? It's *not* floating." As you continue with the activity, make sure your toddler gets plenty of opportunities to drop items into the water to help hold her interest.

Preschooler and School-Age Child

Discuss with your preschooler and school-age child why certain items float and others sink. What do they think the reason is? Let them discover that even if items weigh the same, they may not float or sink the same. For example, have them test this fact with a wooden block and a steel fork. What do they think will happen? Are their predictions correct?

Parent Tip
To introduce the concepts of sinking and floating, read *Who Sank the Boat?* by Pamela Allen with your children.

Food Pyramids

Make colorful food pyramids to teach your kids about healthy eating.

What You'll Need	All Ages	Baby	Toddler	Preschooler	School-Age Child
5 large sheets of construction paper, each in one of these colors: orange, green, red, blue, and purple	🖐				
Markers	🖐				
Grocery flyers and magazines	🖐				
Child-safe scissors	🖐				
Glue sticks	🖐				
Large sheet of yellow construction paper					🖐

Fold and cut each sheet of construction paper in half diagonally to create ten pyramids. Set aside five pyramids, one of each color, to use in other activities (such as "A Shapely Mural" on page 222). Label the remaining pyramids with the following food group names, coordinating the labels with the colors used in the United States Department of Agriculture (USDA) MyPyramid food guidance system:

- Grains (orange)
- Vegetables (green)

- Fruits (red)
- Milk (blue)
- Meat and Beans (purple)

Once the pyramids are ready, take a few minutes to discuss each food group with your children. For example, you may say, "The milk group not only includes the milk we drink but also foods made from milk, like yogurt and cheese." Together, look through grocery flyers and magazines for pictures of foods, helping your kids determine which items belong in which groups. Finally, have them cut out the images and glue each onto the appropriate pyramid.

Baby and Toddler

Team up with your baby and toddler for this activity, which can be a great vocabulary builder. As you find and cut out images, hold up each one and say what it is and what food group it belongs to. For example, you can show them a picture of an apple and say, "This is an apple. It's a fruit." Then spread the glue on the back of the image and let your toddler press it onto the correct pyramid.

Preschooler

Challenge your preschooler to find images to fill certain pyramids. For example, say to him, "We need another picture for our vegetable pyramid. Can you find a vegetable?" Or have him find specific images that make up a balanced diet, such as dark green or orange vegetables.

School-Age Child

As a special assignment, make a yellow pyramid and label it
"Oils." Oils aren't a true food group, but they're still an important part of nutrition. Explain to your school-age child that a
healthy diet includes small amounts of vegetable oils or oils
from natural sources such as fish, nuts, olives, and avocadoes.
Challenge her to find images for this special pyramid.

Parent Tip
Display the finished pyramids in the kitchen, and have your
children put small star stickers next to foods they've tried at
least once. This exercise may encourage them to earn more
stars by trying the foods they've been avoiding!

Phone Book Fun

Let your children have some fun with an old phone book before recycling it.

What You'll Need	All Ages	Baby	Toddler	Preschooler	School-Age Child
Old phone book	🖐				
Crayon			🖐		
Highlighter				🖐	
Watch or timer					🖐

Divide an old phonebook into sections, one for each child, by opening the book flat and ripping along the spine. Give a section to each child, and let them have fun exploring the pages in different ways.

Baby

If your baby is six months or older, give her a page or two to crumple in her fist. She'll love the paper's texture and the crinkling sound it makes! If your baby is younger, crumple the pages for her. You may also want to gently fan her with a few pages. She'll enjoy the cool breeze.

Toddler

Your toddler will love ripping out the phone book pages. When she has torn out some pages, help her find the first letter of her name on them. Circle each find with a crayon and say something such as, "There's a *B*. *B* is for Brooke. That's you! Can you find another *B*?"

Preschooler

You can challenge your preschooler by calling out a random number for him to find in the phone book. For example, ask him to find the number 4, then have him use a highlighter to mark all the 4s he can find on one page. This phone book activity is the perfect time to have him recite his own phone number and even practice dialing it.

School-Age Child

Your school-age child can practice his alphabetization skills with his phone book section. Point out the words or names at the top of each page, and explain that they are the first and last entries on that page. Then have him rip out a number of pages, mix them up, and put them back into alphabetical order. If you like, time him, then challenge him to mix up the pages again and try to beat his time.

Make a Rainbow

Dazzle your children by using simple science to create an indoor rainbow!

What You'll Need	All Ages	Baby	Toddler	Preschooler	School-Age Child
Compact mirror	🖐				
Empty clear glass jar	🖐				
Pitcher of water	🖐				
Flashlight	🖐				
Crayons, markers, and construction paper			🖐	🖐	🖐

Gather a compact mirror, clear glass jar, pitcher of water, and flashlight, and head to a darkened room with your children. (A room with light-colored walls will let your kids see rainbows the best.) Place the compact mirror, titled slightly upward, into the jar. Help your preschooler pour water into the jar, then have your school-age child shine a flashlight though the water and onto the mirror. A rainbow will appear on the wall opposite the mirror. If one doesn't, change the angle of the flashlight or mirror. Your children can enjoy the rainbow in the following age-appropriate ways:

- Hold your baby close to the rainbow so he can see the array of colors. (That is, if being in a dark room doesn't lull him to sleep!)

- Encourage your toddler to touch the rainbow. Depending on where it is, she may need to reach high and jump, or she'll need to crouch low.
- Ask your preschooler to identify the shape of the rainbow and name the colors she sees in it.
- Challenge your school-age child to change the angle of the mirror or shine the flashlight at a different angle to make rainbows in other locations around the room.
- Discuss the "magic" behind making a rainbow: Light is made up of all the colors. When water mixes with light, it acts as a prism, which means it breaks the light into seven main colors: red, orange, yellow, green, blue, indigo, and violet.
- Discuss how the indoor rainbow is similar to and different from the rainbow they see in the sky after it rains.
- Follow up by having your toddler, preschooler, and school-age child draw their own rainbows with crayons or markers.

Name Plates

What's in a name? Your children can find out during this fun activity.

What You'll Need	All Ages	Baby	Toddler	Preschooler	School-Age Child
Child-safe scissors	✋				
Construction paper	✋				
Baby name book	✋				
Crayons and stickers	✋				
Clear contact paper	✋				

Help your children cut out 3-inch-by-9-inch rectangles from construction paper. With the help of a baby name book, like one of the many by Bruce Lansky (Meadowbrook Press), write the meaning of each child's name along the bottom of a rec-tangle, then write the child's name above the meaning in larger letters. (Your older children may do this step themselves or with some help.) Your toddler, preschooler, and school-age child can then decorate their name plates and the baby's with crayons and stickers.

When each name plate is done, cover both sides with clear contact paper and trim the excess. You can use the name plates to label shelf space or toy boxes, assign seats at the dining table, and more!

Baby

Your baby's name is one of the first words he'll recognize and understand. Introduce him to the written form of his name by tracing his finger over the letters on his name plate.

Toddler

This activity is a good one to introduce writing to your toddler. Have him write his name on his name plate with your help. Show him how to hold a crayon between his thumb and index finger, then guide his hand with your own as you write his name. Make sure to identify each letter as you write it with him.

Preschooler

Your preschooler may need help spelling his name. If he does, write it on a scrap of construction paper so he can use it as a guide. When he's ready to decorate his name plate, encourage him to draw objects that begin with each letter of his name. For example, if his name is Jack, ask him to draw a jet, apple, cat, and key.

School-Age Child

If you like, put your school-age child in charge of finding her and her siblings' names in the baby name book. Have her read the meanings to you, or she can write them on the name plates herself. Encourage her to share with her siblings whatever she discovers about their names.

Head, Shoulders, Knees, and Toes

Here's a fun, well-known song that teaches your kids about their bodies.

What You'll Need	All Ages	Baby	Toddler	Preschooler	School-Age Child
Blanket		✋			

Use the following song to teach your kids about the different parts of their bodies.

Head, shoulders, knees, and toes,
knees and toes.
Head, shoulders, knees, and toes,
knees and toes.
Eyes and ears
and mouth and nose.
Head, shoulders, knees, and toes,
knees and toes.

Each time a body part is mentioned, encourage your older children to touch or point to the corresponding part. Below you'll find other age-appropriate ways to enjoy the song.

Baby

Help your baby learn about his body through infant massage. This technique benefits both baby and parent as it gives special time for bonding, promotes relaxation, and may improve your baby's sleep. Lay him on his back on a blanket and sing the song, using your fingertips to gently rub his scalp and massage his shoulders, knees, and toes.

Toddler

At about thirteen months old, your toddler may be able to identify one body part. At about eighteen months old, she may identify up to six body parts. Before singing, help her identify her head, shoulders, knees, and toes. For example, ask her, "Where is your head? It's right here!" (Point to her head.) "Where are your toes? That's right. There they are!" (Point to her toes.)

Preschooler

Most preschoolers can identify the major parts of their bodies. After singing "Head, Shoulders, Knees, and Toes" a few times, make it fun by speeding up or by changing a body part to touch. For instance, sing, "Head, shoulders, knees, and elbows."

School-Age Child

Your school-age child is ready to learn about the internal parts of her body. Discuss the many systems in her body, including cardiovascular, respiratory, nervous, and digestive, and name some of the main organs in each system. Then sing these new lyrics and challenge her to place her hand over the corresponding body parts:

Brain, stomach, heart, and lungs,
heart and lungs.
Brain, stomach, heart, and lungs,
heart and lungs.
Throat and tongue—
all inside.
Brain, stomach, heart, and lungs,
heart and lungs.

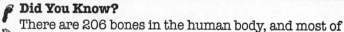

> **Did You Know?**
> There are 206 bones in the human body, and most of them are in the hands and feet.

Let's Go to the Library

There's nothing better than visiting your local library with your children!

What You'll Need	All Ages	Baby	Toddler	Preschooler	School-Age Child
A love of books!	✋				

Whether it's your first trip to the library as a family or your hundredth, here are some ways to make it a fun, educational experience.

Baby

When visiting the library, ask a librarian for the staff's recommendations for babies. You'll discover some wonderful titles! It's important to read to your baby every day. Hearing the stories will help his language development, and snuggling together makes reading time special. If your baby is around six months old, he can help choose a book to check out. Hold up two brightly colored books and see which one he moves toward.

Toddler

Toddlerhood is a busy, important time. Your toddler will greatly benefit from books that feature other kids and how they deal with real issues such as using the potty or sleeping in a big bed. His vocabulary is also growing tremendously and can be reinforced through reading together. Be sure to check out books that discuss the events and issues in his life, plus let him choose a few board books about objects or characters he's currently into, like trains or ducks.

Preschooler

Before visiting the library, ask your preschooler what she wants to learn more about. For example, if dinosaurs fascinate her, encourage her to look for books about dinosaurs. To help her further understand how the library can be a learning resource, help her ask a librarian for book suggestions on her favorite topics.

School-Age Child

Your school-age child can find books on her own. Show her how to use the library's electronic catalog to locate books by call number, then show her how find the number by reading the labels on the bookcases and shelves. After finding her own books, she can help younger siblings find books that interest them.

Money! Money! Money!

It is never too early to discuss money with children. A great way to get started is to have them create their own banks.

What You'll Need	All Ages	Baby	Toddler	Preschooler	School-Age Child
Coins	✋				
Empty plastic bottles		✋			✋
Empty milk cartons			✋	✋	
Construction paper			✋	✋	
Glue sticks			✋	✋	
Scissors			✋	✋	
Stickers			✋		
Markers				✋	✋
Masking tape					✋

Baby

Let your baby watch as you or an older child drops coins into a empty plastic bottle. Name each coin (quarter, dime, nickel, and penny) as you do so. Once the bottle is securely closed, allow her to shake it and see the coins move about.

Toddler

Help your toddler make his own bank. Cover an empty milk carton with construction paper, cut a slit for the coins, and let him decorate it with stickers. When he's done, he'll have fun dropping coins into the bank. Teach him how to open the carton to release the coins and start all over again. *Note*: Close parental supervision is required because coins pose a choking risk.

Preschooler
Your preschooler can also make a bank from a milk carton. Cover the carton with construction paper, cut a slit, and let him decorate his bank any way he chooses. Or if he wants to make a fire truck bank, use red construction paper and have him draw wheels, windows, and a ladder with a black marker. To make a dog bank, use brown construction paper and have him draw a face on it. You could even attach a long strip of brown construction paper as a tail. Before having him add coins to his bank, help him sort them by value.

School-Age Child
Is your school-age child earning money for completing chores around the house? (See "Helping Hands" on page 236 for ideas about age-appropriate chores.) If so, experts recommend teaching children how to deal with money responsibly. Provide her with three bottles: Label one for spending, one for saving, and one for charity. She can cover her bottles with masking tape and then color them with markers. At the end of each month, she can go shopping with her spending money and decide where to send her donation.

A Shapely Mural

Your children can use all sorts of cut-out shapes to make a mural.

What You'll Need	All Ages	Baby	Toddler	Preschooler	School-Age Child
Pencil	👋				
Child-safe scissors	👋				
Construction paper in various colors	👋				
Tape	👋				
Large sheet of paper (or poster board)	👋				
Glue sticks			👋	👋	👋

Begin by helping your children draw and cut out various geometric shapes from different-colored construction paper. Then tape a sheet of paper (or poster board) to the wall or lay it on a table where everyone can reach it. Have your kids arrange the cut-out shapes into objects, scenes, or designs, then have them glue the shapes onto the paper. When finished, this mural will make a creative backdrop in a playroom or other prominent place.

Baby

While his siblings work on the mural, hold up some of the cut-out shapes and describe them to him. For example, say, "This is a square, and this is a triangle." Put the shapes on his high-chair tray and guide his finger around them. He will also enjoy watching the mural come together with its bright, contrasting colors and shapes.

Toddler

Help your toddler identify the various shapes, and encourage her to add them to the mural. For example, ask her, "Can you find a circle and help me glue it onto the mural?" Cover the shape with glue and let her decide where to place it on the mural. You may also want to challenge her to find cutouts by shape as well as color: "Can you find a blue triangle?"

Preschooler

Challenge your preschooler to create a scene with the shapes. For example, he can use three circles to make a snowman next to a square house with a triangle roof. He may want to arrange the shapes on the floor or table first, then glue them onto the mural.

School-Age Child

Encourage your school-age child to re-create a family memory, like sledding or drinking hot cocoa with her siblings, with the shapes. For instance, she can use a rectangle to make a sled or a square with an oval on top to create a mug of hot cocoa. Have her write a description of the memory next to her artwork.

CHAPTER 7

Team Family

I remember the first time my husband and I witnessed our kids getting along and helping each other out. This miracle may be one of our proudest moments as parents!

—Heather

Somewhere in the midst of the hustle and bustle of family life, your children learn to work together and truly bond. That's what this chapter focuses on. Whether these activities encourage your kids to cooperate while doing household chores or celebrate one another's birthdays, they'll teach your children what it means to be a family. Your kids will discover how they're each an important part of the family, but they'll also discover how they're each important to one another.

Me and My Family Scrapbook

Your children will love to make a scrapbook that celebrates them!

What You'll Need	All Ages	Baby	Toddler	Preschooler	School-Age Child
Family photos (or copies)	✋				
Construction paper	✋				
Glue sticks	✋				
Markers			✋	✋	✋
Stickers			✋	✋	✋
Stapler	✋				
Clear contact paper		✋			

Before doing this activity, gather photos of your children. You'll want to make sure there are at least three to four photos of each child, as well as a few family images. Each child will use photos of himself for his own scrapbook page. If you want to preserve the originals, make copies. When it's time for the activity, give your children each several sheets of construction paper. Help them glue the photos onto the front and back of each page. If your children like, they can add a caption under each photo and decorate the pages with markers and stickers. After your children finish their pages, stack them then staple them together along the left side to create a book.

Baby

Hold your baby in your lap as you create her scrapbook pages. While you glue photos onto the paper, tell her about what's going on in them. If your baby is older than six months, choose a few additional photos of her family, glue them onto a separate sheet of paper, then cover the sheet with clear contact paper. Give the sheet to her so she can see the images of her loved ones close up.

Toddler

You can help your toddler make his page by dabbing glue on the backs of the photos and letting him press them into place on the paper. Then point to each photo and ask a question such as, "Who is that?" Write his response near the photo even if it's simply "Me!"

Preschooler

Your preschooler will enjoy showcasing her photos. Let her arrange and glue them onto the page as she likes. She can add her own special touches to the page with stickers and markers. Ask her to give you a caption to include near each photo.

School-Age Child

In addition to designing his own scrapbook pages, your school-age child may enjoy creating a special cover page for the book that includes a title. Add the cover to the top of the stack before you staple the pages together.

Our Family Tree

Create a family tree made of real branches and homemade leaves.

What You'll Need	All Ages	Baby	Toddler	Preschooler	School-Age Child
12-inch branch with twigs	✋				
Modeling clay	✋				
Large plastic cup	✋				
Pencils	✋				
Cardstock	✋				
Child-safe scissors	✋				
Green construction paper	✋				
Ink pad		✋			
Crayons	✋				
Stickers	✋				
Paper clips	✋				
Wet wipes		✋			

In your yard or neighborhood, find a 12-inch branch with several small twigs. Place modeling clay at the bottom of a large plastic cup. Stick the branch upright in the cup, using the modeling clay to secure it in place. Next, draw a leaf pattern that's 6 inches long on cardstock, then cut it out. Your preschooler and school-age child can trace the pattern on green construction paper, then cut out the shape to create leaves for themselves and their younger siblings. Your children can then write their names (with help, for the younger ones) on the back of the leaves and decorate the other side with crayons or stickers. Use paper clips to attach each leaf to a twig on the branch to create a family tree.

Baby
Your baby can help create his own leaf. Gently press his thumb onto an ink pad and then onto the leaf several times to create a fun design or even to write his name with thumbprints. Have wet wipes nearby to clean his hand when you're done. While designing his leaf, sing this song to the tune of "I'm a Little Teapot":

I'm a little baby, special and small.
Here is my family; I love them all.
When we add the branches to this tree,
See the names of my family.

Before attaching your baby's leaf to the branch, let him admire the artwork he helped create!

Toddler
Write your toddler's name in big bubble letters on the back of her leaf. If her name is too long to fit, write her initials instead. Say each letter as you write it. Let her use crayons to color in the bubble letters.

Preschooler
After your preschooler has decorated one side of his leaf, help him write his name on the other side. Have him hold a crayon,

then put your hand over his. Print his name on the leaf while guiding his hand so he can practice writing and strengthen his hand movements. Make sure to say each letter as you write it. If your preschooler knows how to write his name, challenge him to write it with bubble letters.

School-Age Child

After she makes her own leaf, your school-age child can make leaves for other family members to complete the family tree. She can create leaves for parents, grandparents, aunts, uncles, and even the family pet!

Parent Tip

If you like, add a decorative touch to the completed family tree: With your children, think up a title for your tree, such as "The Smith Family" or "Our Family Tree." Cut a piece of brightly colored fabric to cover the large plastic cup, and write the title on it with fabric markers. When you're done, glue the fabric around the plastic cup.

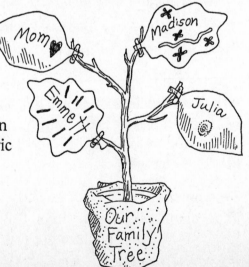

Questions in the Jar

Make mealtime a special time to reconnect with your family by playing this fun question game.

What You'll Need	All Ages	Baby	Toddler	Preschooler	School-Age Child
Glass jar or plastic container	🖐				
Paper	🖐				
Pen	🖐				

Find a clean, empty glass jar or plastic container to place on the center of your dining room table. On separate slips of paper, write questions about your children's thoughts, interests, and dreams. Here are some examples:

- *What is the best thing about being the age you are?*
- *What would be a perfect day for you?*
- *Who is your favorite friend? Why?*
- *If you could have any animal as a pet, which would you choose?*
- *If you could take a family vacation anyplace in the world, where would you go?*
- *If you had three wishes, what would they be?*

When done writing questions, put the slips in the jar. At mealtime, have your children take turns picking slips from the jar and answering the questions. In no time, there will be a lively, pleasant conversation at the dinner table!

Baby

Although your baby can't converse verbally, she'll enjoy hearing loved ones' voices and seeing their faces. When it's her turn to draw a slip, you can either answer the question for her or ask your children what they think their sister's answer would be.

Toddler

Your toddler will need some help when it's his turn. Read the question for him, then entice his answer by asking yes-or-no questions about the topic, such as "Do you like puppies? Would you like one as a pet? Do you like kitties, too?" Or instead of asking your toddler the question from the jar, consider asking him simpler questions, such as "Was it cold out today?" "Did you play with a friend today?" or "Did any books you read today have animals in them?" Either way, he'll enjoy demonstrating his growing vocabulary and cognitive skills.

Preschooler and School-Age Child

After your preschooler and school-age child have replied to their respective questions on the slips, ask them additional questions to expand their answers. For example, if your school-age child answers "Alaska" to the question about an ideal vacation spot, you may say, "What do you think Alaska would be like if we went there on a family vacation?"

Start Your Day Right

What needs to happen each morning to get your family up and ready? Create these visual guides and start off each day right!

What You'll Need	All Ages	Baby	Toddler	Preschooler	School-Age Child
Magazines or crayons			🖐	🖐	🖐
Child-safe scissors			🖐	🖐	🖐
Construction paper	🖐				
Glue sticks	🖐				
Photos		🖐			

Work with your children to think up a list of tasks each child must do each morning, like making the bed, brushing teeth and hair, eating breakfast, and putting on shoes. Make sure the tasks are age appropriate. Then have your toddler, preschooler, and school-age child find magazine images that depict their important morning tasks, or you can help them draw the images. With your help, each child can cut out and glue her images onto a sheet of construction paper to make a guide. Post the guides in a spot where your kids can see them every morning. They can use the guides to get these tasks done quickly while having fun!

Baby

While your baby's siblings make their guides, find photos of her eating, playing, or getting dressed. Show her each photo as you tell her about it. Then glue the photos onto a sheet of construction paper and hang it next to her siblings' guides. Her guide will remind your older children that she has many tasks to complete, just as they do!

Toddler

Help your toddler find three pictures that depict his morning routine. Cut out each image, then ask him to tell you what's happening in it: "What is this boy doing? Is he brushing his teeth? Show me how you brush your teeth." Dab glue on the back of each cutout and let your toddler press it onto the construction paper. When finished, point to the images and explain how they make up his morning routine. For example, "When you wake up in the morning, first you brush your teeth, then you eat breakfast and get dressed."

Preschooler

To strengthen your preschooler's sense of sequencing, have him glue his images onto the paper in the proper order. What does he do first? What does he do second? What does he do last? If necessary, here's your chance to try to change his routine! Offer suggestions, such as, "Do you think it may work better if you get dressed after breakfast so if you spill something on your shirt you won't have to change again?"

School-Age Child

As your school-age child prepares to leave for school each morning, her routine may be rushed. When making the guides, encourage her to create a timeline to accompany her images. For example, she can note the hour when she needs to wake up to get things done. She may even want her guide to begin the evening before. For example, she can depict setting out the next day's clothes and note the time when she should do this task the previous night.

> When my son started preschool, we created this guide. Instead of just telling him it was time to get dressed, I could point to the image on the guide and give him a visual cue as well. He liked running to check what task was next.
>
> —Heather

Helping Hands

In this ongoing activity, your children will take pride in jobs well done.

What You'll Need	All Ages	Baby	Toddler	Preschooler	School-Age Child
Construction paper	✋				
Crayons	✋				
Child-safe scissors	✋				
Envelopes	✋				
Tape	✋				

To begin this activity, have your children each place a hand on a sheet of construction paper, then trace around the hand. With your older children's help, cut out the tracings and use each one to create at least five more hand cutouts per child. Place each set of hand cutouts in a separate labeled envelope.

Explain to your children that the cutouts are "helping hands," which represent times when the children have been helpful to someone. Every time a child does a helpful act, you'll tape one of his or her hand cutouts to the wall, refrigerator door, or other highly visible place. Start awarding "helping hands" by recalling a helpful act each child did recently. For example, you may say to your school-age child, "Remember the time you helped change the baby's diaper? That was very helpful." After acknowledging the helpful act, record it on one of his hand cutouts and tape it to the wall. Encourage your children to acknowledge one another's helpful acts over the next few days and continue to add cutouts to the wall. By seeing all their "helping hands," your children will understand how much their contributions help the family.

Baby

Although your baby can't help in the same ways her older siblings can, she can make her family feel loved and special by snuggling, cooing, smiling, or even listening intently. Be sure to point out your baby's helpful contributions to her siblings. For example, if your preschooler seems out of sorts, you can say to him, "See the baby smiling at you? She wants you to be happy, too!" Your baby's hand cutouts will make great keepsakes as well as chart her development.

Toddler

At this age, toddlers are beginning to empathize and sympathize with others. If your toddler sees a sibling cry, she may try to help by offering her teddy bear, a hug, or just a caring glance. To help her understand the connection between receiving a hand cutout and doing a helpful act, tell her why she's earned a "helping hand." For example, "You made your sister feel better by giving her a hug." Also verbalize your helpful actions to her. For example, "I'm giving your brother a hug because he's feeling sad."

Preschooler

Most preschoolers like to exert their newfound independence. At this point, they can dress themselves, put on their shoes, and even make their beds. Your preschooler is at the perfect age to assist his younger siblings with these tasks. Encourage him to help a younger sibling learn to pull on socks or take off shoes.

School-Age Child

Your school-age child may be ready to help in more involved ways. For example, you can suggest that he set the table, fold laundry, or feed the dog. Challenge him to come up with other ways he can help.

Parent Tip

Long after this activity is over, continue to acknowledge your children's helpful acts with a round of applause, a high-five, or a hug and kiss. You may also want to rustle their hair, rub their backs, or hold their hands. Your kids will love the attention and appreciation!

Family Letter

Work with your children to write a family letter to send to someone special.

What You'll Need	All Ages	Baby	Toddler	Preschooler	School-Age Child
Paper, pencil, envelope, and stamp	🖐				
Scale and tape measure		🖐			
Ink pad		🖐			
Wet wipes		🖐			
Stickers			🖐	🖐	
Crayons				🖐	

Gather around the kitchen table and tell your children you're going to write a family letter. To get started, brainstorm about your children's accomplishments and news. Ask each child questions such as "What makes you happy?" and "What have you learned to do that makes you proud?" Write down their answers. Your children can then help you create a family letter to mail to someone they love.

Baby

Your baby can't express himself verbally, so let his siblings answer your questions about his accomplishments. The recipient of the letter will surely want to know how much your baby has grown, so let your children help you weigh and measure their brother with a scale and tape measure. Encourage your older kids to give him lots of hugs and kisses as they take his measurements. He'll love the attention! Have him "sign" the finished letter with a handprint. Press the palm side of his hand onto an ink pad, then press it onto the letter. Have wet wipes nearby for cleanup.

Toddler

Make sure to ask your toddler open-ended questions as well as yes-or-no questions. For example, ask her, "What did you do today?" and "Do you want to tell Grandma about your favorite toy?" This exercise will build his vocabulary. You may also want to let your toddler decorate the back of the envelope with stickers.

Preschooler

Your preschooler may enjoy talking at length about all her accomplishments. Challenge her to narrow her answers to just the most important ones. After the questions, she can contribute to the letter in many ways: She can decorate the border of the finished letter with crayons and stickers, and she may be able to print her own name to sign it. If she likes, she can draw a portrait of her and her siblings to include with the letter. Finally, let her place the stamp on the envelope in the appropriate space.

School-Age Child

Your school-age child may enjoy writing the letter using the answers you recorded (with your help, if needed). Explain to her the basic parts of a formal letter: the date, the greeting, the main body, and a closing with everyone's names. Tell her where to write each part.

Parent Tip
This activity is a great opportunity to review your home address with your children.

Show Me a Sign

Show your children how to communicate without saying a word!

What You'll Need	All Ages	Baby	Toddler	Preschooler	School-Age Child
Hands!	✋				
ASL resource, such as a dictionary or website	✋				

Many parents use American Sign Language (ASL) to communicate with their children. See the chart on page 244 for signs to identify family members, but feel free to consult an ASL resource to learn more. Repeat each sign several times as you say the corresponding word.

Baby

Babies can control their hand movements before they can speak, and they can recognize a sign well before they start using it on their own. These facts mean you can start using signs with your baby from birth. In addition to the signs on page 244, other important signs you may wish to teach your baby include:

- *More*: Bring fingertips of both hands together and tap lightly.
- *Milk*: Open and close your right hand repeatedly as if milking a cow.

- *Eat*: Touch the fingertips and thumb of your right hand to your lips.
- *Drink*: Form a C shape with your right hand, then bring it up in a short arc to your mouth as if drinking from a glass.

Toddler

Sign language will build your toddler's growing vocabulary. Sign often around her and encourage her to sign, too. For example, point to the baby and ask, "Who is this? Can you tell me with a sign?"

Preschooler

Using sign language requires preschoolers to look at the person communicating with them, which may help them pay attention. Practice signing with your preschooler in everyday communication. For instance, you may ask him, "Can you get a toy for your...?" Then sign *brother*. As your preschooler masters making the signs, challenge him to come up with more signs to learn.

School-Age Child

In the signing community, each person makes a sign to represent his or her name. Encourage your school-age child to create a sign to represent her name. She may also enjoy learning the sign language alphabet. You can find the signs for each letter in your ASL resource. After she's learned the signs for the letters, challenge her to spell some words using the signs.

Word	How to Make the Sign
Mommy	With an open hand, touch your thumb to your chin and wiggle your fingers slightly.
Daddy	With an open hand, touch your thumb to your forehead and wiggle your fingers slightly.
Brother	Grasp the brim of an imaginary cap with your thumb and fingers.
Sister	Tuck the fingers of your hand, touch that thumb to your cheek, and sweep the thumb down the side of your face to your chin.
Baby	Sway your arms together as if rocking a baby.

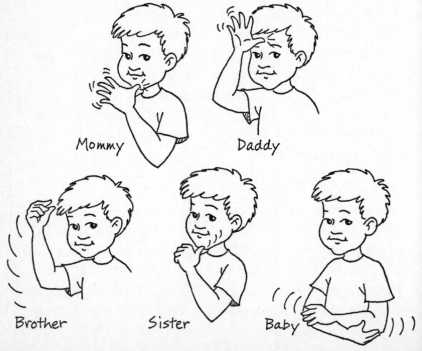

Mommy   Daddy

Brother   Sister   Baby

A Royal Birthday Throne

This easy-to-do project is a great way to make your children feel like kings and queens on their birthdays!

What You'll Need	All Ages	Baby	Toddler	Preschooler	School-Age Child
Decoration supplies, such as streamers, paper, tape, crayons, stickers, tempera paint, child-safe scissors, and so on	✋				

On each child's birthday, let the other children make a throne so the birthday child can receive the royal treatment. Choose a chair appropriate for the birthday child, then give your children various supplies to decorate the chair. If they need direction, prompt them to consider the birthday child's favorite colors, cartoon characters, or nursery rhymes as decoration ideas. Below are some age-appropriate suggestions for how each child can help decorate the throne. *Note*: We strongly advise not using balloons for this activity. They pose a serious choking risk to children.

Baby

Your baby can add the perfect decoration for a sibling's birthday throne: If a sibling is turning three, paint and press three of the baby's fingers onto a sheet of paper. If a sibling is turning eight, use eight fingers. You can cut out the imprint and glue this decoration onto the throne.

Toddler

Tear off 12-inch pieces of streamer for your toddler to decorate. Lay them on the table and tape down the ends. He can cover the pieces with stickers, then help you attach them to the birthday child's chair. Let him decide where they should go.

Preschooler

What is the birthday child's favorite activity or animal? How about a favorite food or friend? Have your preschooler draw a picture of the favorite thing to tape to the birthday child's chair.

School-Age Child

Your school-age child can print the birthday child's name in fancy lettering or write a special birthday message on a sheet of paper, then tape it to the back of the chair.

Parent Tip

If possible, try to make the throne a surprise for the birthday child. Have his siblings decorate the chair beforehand, then hide it until his birthday! You may also want to create a special crown for the birthday child (see "King and Queen Crowns" on page 304).

Time Capsule

Create a time capsule to capture this time in your children's lives!

What You'll Need	All Ages	Baby	Toddler	Preschooler	School-Age Child
Plastic, metal, or heavy-duty rubber container (roughly the size of an adult shoebox)	🖐				
Roll of ribbon and scissors	🖐				
Bathroom scale	🖐				
Index cards and markers	🖐				
Construction paper and crayons	🖐				

Explain to your children that a time capsule is something to store fun and unique mementos that describe what a person or community is like right now. On a certain date, you open the time capsule and see how much things have changed! To get started, choose a small container as your capsule, then work with your children to create special mementos. On the next page you'll find some recommendations.

After your time capsule is full of mementos, seal it and decide together when it will be reopened. Kids grow and change quickly, but at least several months should pass so your children can easily see how much they've changed since making the time capsule. The longer you wait, the more dramatic the changes will be. Once you choose a reopening date, tell them you will store the capsule in an out-of-the-way place until then. We recommend in your attic, basement, or garage. (Just make sure to write down its location!)

Height and Weight
Use a roll of ribbon to measure each child's height from head to toe. Cut the ribbon and write the child's name on it. Use a bathroom scale to record your children's weights on separate index cards.

Special Skills or Characteristics
Record your children's latest skills or characteristics on separate index cards. For example, record how high your toddler can count and how many teeth your baby has. And also record what makes each child unique, such as "He laughs when Daddy scratches his belly!"

Favorites
Record your children's favorite toys, songs, stories, foods, or other items on separate index cards. Your preschooler may enjoy drawing pictures of the favorites on the cards.

Handprint
Trace each child's hand on construction paper. If you like, cut out the tracings and let your children decorate the cutouts with crayons. Be sure to label each with the date and appropriate name.

Show-and-Tell Me

Let your children show their pride and knowledge with a rousing round of show-and-tell.

What You'll Need	All Ages	Baby	Toddler	Preschooler	School-Age Child
Special objects			✋	✋	✋
Timer	✋				

Invite your children to each find a special object for show-and-tell with their siblings. It may be a toy, book, souvenir, art project, or collectible. You should grab an object, too. Gather in a circle. To demonstrate how to "show-and-tell," hold up your object for everyone to see, then tell them about where you got it and why it's so special to you. Have your children take turns showing and telling about their special objects.

Baby

When it's your baby's turn to show, let her show off a new skill. For example, has she learned sign language? Can she smile on cue? Blow a raspberry? Sit up on her own or pick up a piece of cereal? For the "telling" part, you can share your memories of when each of your older children first began doing the particular skill.

Toddler
When it's your toddler's turn to show, ask him to demonstrate ways he plays with, uses, or enjoys his object. Encourage him to tell everyone about his special object by asking a few yes-or-no questions. For example, "Do you love that toy? Do you sleep with that toy? Did Daddy buy that toy at the store?"

Preschooler
Your preschooler will have no problem showing off her special object and telling her siblings all about it. When it's her siblings' turns, however, teach her how to be a good listener and encourage her to ask thoughtful questions. Model this behavior by asking the speaker, "You mentioned that someone who is very special bought this bear for you. Who is that special person?" Then prompt your preschooler by saying, "Did your brother mention something you want to hear more about?"

School-Age Child
For a twist on show-and-tell, challenge your school-age child to show off a skill he can do, then tell his siblings how to do it. For example, if he plays soccer, he can show his moves with his soccer ball, then teach his siblings how to do the tricks.

Let's All Pitch In

This activity shows your children that families who work together, play together!

What You'll Need	All Ages	Baby	Toddler	Preschooler	School-Age Child
Large sheet of paper	👋				
Crayons	👋				
Magazines, child-safe scissors, and glue sticks				👋	👋
Tape	👋				
Medium-size jar	👋				
Cotton balls	👋				

Write each child's name at the top of a large sheet of paper. With your children, think of chores or tasks each can do. (See age-appropriate suggestions on the next page.) Write each task under the appropriate child's name. If you like, your older children can draw pictures of the tasks (or glue magazine images that depict them) as visual cues for the younger children. When the chart is ready, tape it in a prominent place.

Then find a medium-size jar and place it next to the chart. Tell your children that each time they complete a task, you'll give them a cotton ball to put into the Family Fun Jar. When the jar is full, they can help make plans for a special family event, like a trip to the zoo or the movies!

Baby

Your baby can't help with chores, but you and your older children can "assign" other important tasks like trying to roll over, eating a new food, burping after a feeding, or even smiling or cooing. Your baby will love the attention he'll receive from his siblings as they watch for these accomplishments.

Toddler

Toddlers love to mimic others, and your toddler may often mimic you as you do household chores. Use this activity to show her simple chores she can do. For example, if you show her how to put away her toys in the toy box or stack her board books, she'll likely join in.

Preschooler

Your preschooler can help you come up with chores and tasks just for him. Self-help skills are an important part of a preschooler's life as he learns to work independently from you. For example, he can get dressed by himself or hang up his coat. He can also strip his bed when it's time to wash the bedding.

School-Age Child

Your school-age child can use this opportunity to think of new ways she can help around the home. If she needs direction, give her an example, such as emptying the wastebaskets, setting the dinner table, or feeding the family pet. Also encourage her to take on the important task of showing a younger child how to do an age-appropriate chore.

Get-Well Basket

Have your children cheer up a sick sibling with a thoughtful get-well basket.

What You'll Need	All Ages	Baby	Toddler	Preschooler	School-Age Child
Basket	✋				
Basket goodies (see next page for examples)	✋				
Small cotton blanket	✋				
Fabric markers	✋				
Ribbon	✋				

Show your children an empty basket and tell them they're going to fill it with goodies that will cheer up a sibling when he or she isn't feeling well. Have your children use their imaginations to decide what goodies to include in the basket. Ask them what things would make them feel better if they were sick. Challenge them to come up with ideas any sibling of any age will appreciate, or encourage them to have a balance of younger and older items.

After deciding what goodies to include, have your kids collect the items, then help you arrange them in the basket. Next, have your children decorate a small cotton blanket with fabric markers. You can trace your baby's hand on the blanket, your toddler can doodle on it, your preschooler can draw a smiley face, and your school-age child can write well-wishes or a comforting message. When the ink is dry, wrap the basket in the blanket, tie it closed with a ribbon, and store the basket. Plan to present the basket as a family whenever one of your children is sick.

Parent Tip
Remind your children that the items in the basket will be stored away until someone is sick. Therefore, they shouldn't include items they use or want on a regular basis, such as a beloved toy or frequently watched DVD.

Basket Goodies
Tissues
Plush animal
Quiet toy
CD of relaxing music
Special DVD
Coloring book and crayons
Bell: The sick sibling can ring the bell from his bed or the couch when he needs something. (See page 116 for a homemade variety.)
IOUs: Sick kids always feel as though they're missing out on things. With these IOUs, your children can give their sick sibling something to look forward to when he feels better. They can write "IOU a game of tag" or "IOU a chance to borrow one of my toys."

CHAPTER 8
World Family

I took out a map the other day to show my kids where I was heading on a business trip. "We're here," I said, pointing to Massachusetts. "And I'm going here." I moved my finger over a few inches to point to Arkansas. They looked puzzled, as I knew they would. Finally, my son asked, "But why do you even have to take a plane there?"

—Heather

Most children don't realize there's a big, wide world beyond their own horizon. They also don't realize their actions can make this world a better place. In this chapter, your children will learn about different lands, cultures, and languages. Most importantly, they'll also learn about contributing to the world in special ways by showing compassion and respect for all living things. It's never too early to expand your children's views.

Hello and Goodbye!

Introduce new cultures to your children through different languages!

What You'll Need	All Ages	Baby	Toddler	Preschooler	School-Age Child
Plush animal			🖐		
World atlas or globe				🖐	🖐

Young children learn foreign languages quicker than teens and adults, so teach your children how to say "hello" and "goodbye" in different languages. See the next page for a list of these words and their pronunciations. Feel free to add other languages to your list. If your child is learning a foreign language at school, encourage him to teach his siblings other simple words in that language.

Baby

Waving "bye-bye" is one of the first gestures babies learn. Show your baby how to wave goodbye in another language. For example, make eye contact with him, then wave your hand while saying, "*Adiós!*" or "*Sayonara!*"

Toddler

Play a fun game with your toddler to help him learn foreign words. Hold a plush animal in front of him. As you hide it from his view, say "goodbye" in one of the languages. Then say "hello" in that language while quickly bringing the animal back in his view. Do these actions again and again, encouraging him to say the appropriate words. He may not pronounce them correctly, but he'll enjoy saying them as part of the game.

Preschooler and School-Age Child
Teach your older children the foreign words on the list, then use this activity to strengthen geography and role-playing skills. Provide a world atlas or globe and point to a country whose people speak a language listed below. For example, point to France and say to one child, "Pretend you're buying bread from your brother the baker. What will you say to each other?" Encourage your children to say the appropriate foreign words during the scene. For example, your child can say to her brother, "*Bonjour*! I would like to buy some bread."

Hello and Goodbye in Other Languages				
Language	Hello	Pronunciation	Goodbye	Pronunciation
Chinese	*Ni hao*	(NEE-how)	*Zaijian*	(dzeye-zhee-EN)
French	*Bonjour*	(bone-ZHOOR)	*Au revior*	(oh reh-VWAHR)
German	*Guten Tag*	(GOO-tun tahk)	*Auf Wiedersehen*	(owf VEE-der-zayn)
Italian	*Buon giorno*	(bwone JOHR-noh)	*Arrivederci*	(ah-ree-vah-DARE-chee)
Japanese	*Domo*	(DOH-moh)	*Sayonara*	(sigh-YOH-nah-rah)
Spanish	*Buenos dias*	(bway-nohs DEE-ahs)	*Adiós*	(ah-DYOHS)
Swedish	*God dag*	(goo dog)	*Adjö*	(ahd-YOH)

Feed All the Little Birds

Your children can take care of their feathered friends with these simple birdfeeders.

What You'll Need	All Ages	Baby	Toddler	Preschooler	School-Age Child
Round cereal with holes, like Cheerios or Froot Loops	🖐				
Bowls			🖐	🖐	🖐
Pipe cleaners	🖐				
Yarn and scissors			🖐	🖐	🖐

Pour the cereal into separate bowls for your toddler, preschooler, and school-age child. Show your children how to string the cereal onto a pipe cleaner to make a hanging birdfeeder. When done, twist each end of the pipe cleaner to make a loop. Then use yarn to tie the birdfeeders to the branches of nearby trees.

Baby

If your baby is eating cereal, place a few pieces on her high-chair tray and let her practice grasping them. She'll see her siblings working with the cereal, so she'll want to pick it up, too. If your baby isn't eating solids yet, rub a pipe cleaner on the soles of her feet for a fuzzy sensation!

Toddler

This activity is a perfect chance for your toddler to work on his small motor skills, like picking up a small cereal piece and stringing it onto the pipe cleaner. When it's time to hang your toddler's birdfeeder, secure it near a window, if possible. She'll enjoy watching the birds eat her work.

Preschooler

Give your preschooler colorful cereal to string onto his pipe cleaner. Show him how he can make patterns with the pieces. For example, he can string on a blue piece, then a red one, then a blue one, and so on. Encourage him to come up with his own pattern.

School-Age Child

Your school-age child may enjoy making several birdfeeders in different patterns. Encourage him to join his birdfeeders together to create a figure or design to display from a tree branch.

> **Did You Know?**
> Birds use a lot of energy while flying, and many species eat up to 100 percent of their body weight each day to power their flight.

A Birdbath Haven

Birds need reliable access to clean, fresh water, especially in hot weather, so create a homemade birdbath for your yard.

What You'll Need	All Ages	Baby	Toddler	Preschooler	School-Age Child
Old sheet	🖐				
Scissors	🖐				
Sponges	🖐				
Acrylic paint	🖐				
3 medium-size clay pots and a large clay saucer (available at gardening stores)	🖐				
Paper bowls	🖐				
Small aluminum baking dish		🖐			
Bucket			🖐		
Small plastic toy insects	🖐				
Ceramic glue	🖐				
Bird guide					🖐

On a sunny day, lay an old sheet out in the yard for your work-space. Cut sponges into small squares and pour paint into a few paper bowls. Have your toddler, preschooler, and school-age child use the sponges to paint three clay pots and a large clay saucer. When the paint is dry, you and your school-age child can assemble the pieces into a birdbath, and your toddler and preschooler can help put on the final touches (see each age group below). Place the finished birdbath within view of a window in your home. Then watch for birds to take a dip!

Baby

While his siblings create the birdbath, your baby can enjoy playing in his own "birdbath." If your baby can sit up on his own, pour some water in a small aluminum baking dish and let him explore it with his hands. Only use as much water as you are willing to let him get wet! If your baby isn't sitting up yet, hold the dish for him or dab some water on his bare toes with a sponge. When birds visit your yard once the birdbath is finished, be sure to point them out to your baby. The little creatures will fascinate him!

Toddler

Your toddler will enjoy painting with sponges. While the paint dries, assign her to find small rocks to add to the saucer. Have her wash the rocks in a bucket of water before placing them in the birdbath.

Preschooler

When the birdbath is assembled, your preschooler can help you decorate it with plastic insects. He can show you where to glue the insects onto the pots. He can also fill the birdbath with water and make sure it always has a fresh supply.

School-Age Child

Your school-age child can help you assemble the birdbath: Turn one pot upside down. On top of that pot, glue another pot right side up. Then glue the third pot upside down on top of the second pot. Finally, glue the saucer right side up on top of the last pot. When birds begin to visit the birdbath, your school-age child can use a bird guide to identify each species.

Moving around the World

Tour the world's landscapes with this fun action song!

What You'll Need	All Ages	Baby	Toddler	Preschooler	School-Age Child
Voices and bodies!	🖐				

In a room with plenty of open space, sing and act out the following song with your children to the tune of "The Mulberry Bush." Each verse describes a different landscape from around the world.

Here we fly 'round the flat grasslands,
the flat grasslands, the flat grasslands.
Here we fly 'round the flat grasslands
where it is so windy.

(Spin, walk fast, and wave your arms as if being pushed by the wind.)

Here we skate on the polar ice,
the polar ice, the polar ice.
Here we skate on the polar ice
where it is so chilly.

(Move your feet in a skating motion and rub your arms as if cold.)

Here we slide down the sandy dunes,
the sandy dunes, the sandy dunes.
Here we slide down the sandy dunes
in the dry, hot desert.

(Roll on the floor.)

Here we run up the tall mountains,
the tall mountains, the tall mountains.
Here we run up the tall mountains
so we can reach the sky.

(Run in exaggerated motion while reaching arms toward the sky.)

Baby and Toddler

Hold your baby in your arms during this activity and move her body as directed in the song. She'll love listening to her siblings sing and watching them act out the movements! Your toddler will likely be a beat behind the others as he mimics their actions, but that's okay. He'll enjoy doing the movements on his own.

Preschooler and School-Age Child

Have your preschooler and school-age child take turns leading the movements to act out. Challenge them to think of other landscapes to add to the song. For example, they can come up with actions to do on an ocean beach front or valley.

Adopt a Family Tree

Have your children adopt a special tree in your yard or neighborhood. They'll learn a valuable lesson about the beauty of nature.

What You'll Need	All Ages	Baby	Toddler	Preschooler	School-Age Child
A picnic (see "Packin' a Picnic" on page 19 for ideas)	✋				

Prepare a picnic with your children, then take a walk in your yard or in your neighborhood, and together select a tree to "adopt." Sit by the tree and observe its beauty. Ask your children to describe its leaves, trunk, height, and so on. Enjoy the picnic under the foliage. Together, make plans to visit your special tree regularly.

Baby and Toddler
Your baby and toddler will enjoy being outside with their siblings, and their adopted tree will delight their senses. Gently stroke a leaf on your baby's cheek. Encourage your toddler to touch the tree bark with his hands.

Preschooler and School-Age Child
Help your preschooler and school-age child identify the type of tree you've adopted. Discuss the different ways trees benefit the environment. For example, trees provide shade and shelter

to various animals. They also help protect against soil erosion and offset carbon dioxide emissions—important concepts you can begin to explain to your children.

Parent Tip
For added enjoyment, read *The Giving Tree* by Shel Silverstein to your children while under your adopted tree. Afterward, ask them why the tree in the story was so giving. Tell them that by adopting a tree, they'll also be giving.

In addition to visiting your adopted tree, you may also want to care for it. (Be sure to ask permission before tending to a neighborhood tree outside your property). Here are some ways you and your children can care for your adopted tree. Perhaps your children will brainstorm other ideas. Caring for the tree will help develop their nurturing skills as well as help protect the environment!

- Pull weeds from around the trunk and pack fresh soil around the base.
- Water your tree.
- Plant tree seedlings or flowers at the base.
- Chart your tree's growth by periodically taking a family photo in front of it.
- Attract feathered friends to your tree by hanging birdfeeders from its branches. (See page 258.)

Recycling Center

The average American generates more than four pounds of trash every day. That's a lot of garbage! Recycling helps reduce waste and conserve materials, so make a recycling center in your home.

What You'll Need	All Ages	Baby	Toddler	Preschooler	School-Age Child
Markers	🖐				
3 boxes	🖐				
Duct tape	🖐				
Old magazines	🖐				
Child-safe scissors	🖐				
Glue stick	🖐				
3 paper bags	🖐				
Dried beans		🖐			
Empty water bottle		🖐			

Have your older children help you label three boxes "Paper," "Plastic," and "Glass." They can then add visual cues by cutting out magazine images of recyclable items and gluing them onto the appropriate boxes. Attach the boxes in a row with duct tape, then place a paper grocery bag in each box. Explain to your children that it's everyone's responsibility to place recyclable items in the appropriate bags rather than throw them in with the regular garbage. When the bags are full, remove them from the boxes and set them out for collection or bring them to a drop-off site. Then your children can place new bags in the boxes.

Baby

While he watches his siblings work on the recycling center, make a recycled rattle to keep your baby occupied. Place dried beans in an empty water bottle. Be sure to secure the cap tightly. Your baby will enjoy shaking, banging, and rolling his new toy. If he's younger, shake and roll the rattle for him. He'll enjoy listening to the sound.

Toddler, Preschooler, and School-Age Child

Your older children can team up to decorate the boxes. Your school-age child can lead the project by finding images of paper, plastic, and glass items commonly found in your house. Your preschooler can then cut the images and add glue to their backs. Finally, your toddler can stick the images onto the appropriate boxes, with your help. When they're done, send them on a search around the home for any recyclables they can add to the bags right away, such as yesterday's newspaper, an empty soda bottle on the counter, or a near-empty jam jar in the fridge. Help them wash out the items then determine in which bag they each belong.

Parent Tip

Remind your children that the recycling center is a prime location for arts-and-crafts supplies. With activities such as "Recyclables" on page 327, your children can learn how to "recycle" the items to create artwork or practical items.

Charity Roundup

Introduce your children to the satisfaction of helping others in need.

What You'll Need	All Ages	Baby	Toddler	Preschooler	School-Age Child
Donation items (see below)	🖐				
Boxes	🖐				
Blanket		🖐			
Paper towels, tape, glue, and child-safe scissors					🖐
Paper and pencil					🖐

Ask your children to help you gather toys, plush animals, books, games, and clothing they've outgrown or no longer want. Explain in simple terms what you will do with the items. For example: "Won't it be nice to give these things you've out-grown to children who need them?" Your kids can help you sort and box the items, then choose a charitable organization where you can donate them. Congratulate them for giving to others! *Note:* To avoid future tears of regret, don't let your children donate any beloved belongings. Thank them for their generosity, but suggest other toys to donate.

Baby

If your baby is older than six months, she can help pack up the items—and practice her ability to grasp and release. Give her an object she can grab and hold, like a plush animal, and encourage her to release it into a box. If your baby is younger than six months, she can enjoy some tummy time while her siblings work: Lay her on a blanket with a few plush animals nearby. She may exercise her neck muscles to get a look at her furry friends.

Toddler

Play a roundup game with your toddler using the donation items. Describe an object and ask him to get it and drop it in the box. For example, say, "I'm thinking of a toy that's soft and blue. It has a ribbon around its neck. Can you bring that toy to the box?" This exercise will develop his listening skills as well as his vocabulary.

Preschooler

Challenge your preschooler's categorizing skills with a fun activity. Have her sort the items into categories, such as things you wear, things you play with, and all other things. Or have her sort the items by the charities that will receive them. For example, tell her baby items go to one charity, older children's clothing goes to another, and toys go to a third. When she's finished sorting, have her put the items from each category into a separate box.

School-Age child

Because donation items must be in good condition, let your school-age child inspect each item, clean it, and make minor repairs as needed. Give her tools like damp and dry paper towels, tape, glue, and scissors. If an item needs fixing beyond her abilities, have her write a "work order" for you. For example, "Please sew on the bear's eye" or "This shirt has a stain."

Parent Tip

Research local establishments or national charities that accept donations in your area. Here are some ideas:

- Libraries
- Food shelves
- Places of worship
- Shelters
- Hospitals
- Charitable organizations, such as:
    * The Salvation Army (http://www.salvationarmyusa.org)
    * The Home for Little Wanderers (http://www.thehome.org)
    * Goodwill Industries International, Inc. (http://www.goodwill.org)
    * Newborns in Need (http://www.newbornsinneed.org)

Fashion from around the World

Learn about places with different climates, cultures, and traditions by creating these easy-to-make fashions!

What You'll Need	All Ages	Baby	Toddler	Preschooler	School-Age Child
World atlas or globe	✋				
Bath towels		✋		✋	
Old bath towel			✋		
Scissors			✋		
Beach towels					✋

Explain to your children that different people wear different clothing all around the world. On an atlas or globe, point out the following places: Java, Brazil, Alaska, and India. Talk about the different climates and cultures in these places and how that might affect their clothing. Then tell them they're going to create fashions from each of those places. Help your children create their garments, then have them take turns modeling and describing the clothing to one another. Encourage your children to ask questions about their siblings' garments. For example, "Is that comfortable to wear?" Ask them to compare the clothing to the clothing they wear in this culture.

Baby

People in Java wear a sarong, a large sheet of fabric wrapped around the waist and worn as a skirt. Use a bath towel to create a sarong on your baby. He may not tolerate wearing the garment for long, so be sure he's first to display the fashion to his siblings!

Toddler

People in Brazil, especially ranchers, wear a poncho. Make a poncho for your toddler by cutting out a circle large enough for her head from the center of an old bath towel. Slide it over her head and have her pretend to be a rancher galloping around on her horse.

Preschooler

Alaska Native people often wear parkas, which are jackets made from animal fur. To create a parka for your preschooler, wrap a towel over his shoulders and loosely tie a knot to hold it together. Then wrap and tie another towel over his head to make a hood. Centuries ago, people believed that when they wore a parka, they took on the characteristics of the animals from which it was constructed. Encourage your preschooler to act like an Alaskan fur animal, such as a wolf or a mink.

School-Age Child

Women in India often wear a sari. Have your school-age child create this garment by wrapping one end of a beach towel around her waist and draping the other end over her head or one shoulder. Have her walk in the garment—it'll be good practice for posture and balance! Men in India sometimes wear a traditional garment called a *lungi* (pronounced "loon-gee"), a cloth that's draped around the waist. If you like, have your school-age child create and wear that garment.

Parent Tip
This activity is a prime photo opportunity. Have a camera nearby to capture the fashions!

CHAPTER 9
Arts & Crafts

Nearly every inch of my refrigerator door is covered with crayon drawings, glitter-strewn construction paper, and painted handprints. When I have a moment to pause before opening the door, I admire my children's creativity and marvel at how they interpret their world.

—Heather

Children express their creativity as they work side by side on arts-and-crafts projects. In this chapter, your children will discover their own artistic talents as well as one another's. Because art projects can get complicated and messy, we've kept things simple. These activities—which include paper plate self-portraits, water bottle aquariums, and finger paint color wheels—often use the same materials for children of all ages, and we've included specific instructions to bring out the artist in every age group.

Let Me See Your Funny Face

Let your children see all the silly and interesting things they can do with their faces!

What You'll Need	All Ages	Baby	Toddler	Preschooler	School-Age Child
Large mirror	✋				
Old magazines		✋			✋
Child-safe scissors			✋	✋	✋
Colored construction paper			✋	✋	✋
Glue sticks			✋	✋	✋
Paper plates			✋	✋	✋
Stapler					✋

Gather your children around a large mirror to make funny faces and admire their similar and unique features. Then your older children can create self-portraits by gluing construction paper features onto paper plates.

Baby

Your baby will enjoy studying her own face in the mirror. Touch her nose and eyes as she gazes at herself. This action will help her learn that the reflection in the mirror is hers. To strengthen her neck muscles, place her on her tummy in front of the mirror—she'll work hard to get a good look at herself.

While her siblings make funny faces in the mirror, she may even try to mimic them. For more fun, flip through magazines that have lots of close-up photos of faces for her to admire and study.

Toddler

Have your toddler identify the different features of his face, including the colors of his eyes and hair. Cut out eyes, a nose, a mouth, and hair for him from construction paper. Help him glue them onto a paper plate to create his self-portrait.

Preschooler

Your preschooler can cut out eyes, a nose, a mouth, and hair from construction paper for her self-portrait. She may also want to include other facial details like eyebrows, eyelashes, and ears. Your preschooler understands different feelings, too. She may want to create a happy, silly, or tired face. While she works on the project, ask her to identify how she looks similar to or different from her siblings.

School-Age Child

Your school-age child can also use photos from magazines to create a more intricate or silly self-portrait. He can cut out eyes, a nose, and a mouth from images in the magazine. Encourage him to create portraits of his siblings, too, and then staple the paper plates together side by side for a home-made family portrait.

Trace a Place Mat

These fun and functional place mats will teach your children about the objects they need before sitting down for a meal.

What You'll Need	All Ages	Baby	Toddler	Preschooler	School-Age Child
Construction paper	✋				
Child-safe scissors	✋				
Glue sticks	✋				
Plastic plates and cups	✋				
Age-appropriate eating utensils	✋				
Crayons	✋				
Magazines or super-market circulars				✋	

Trace a plate, a cup, and eating utensils onto a sheet of construction paper for your toddler. Your preschooler and school-age child may do this task independently. While you cut out the shapes for your toddler, your older children can cut out their own shapes and glue them onto other sheets of construction paper in the correct places.

Baby

You or your older children can make a special place mat for your baby to explore. After tracing the objects, draw some happy faces on the tracings. For a fun hide-and-seek game, place a plastic plate, cup, and spoon on the correct spaces and see if your baby can find the smiling faces by moving the objects around. If she is younger than six months, her siblings can remove the objects for her while saying, "Peekaboo!"

Toddler
Trace the cutouts onto a blank sheet of construction paper in the proper places for a matching game. Challenge your toddler to compare the cutouts with the tracings on the paper, and then ask him to match them up. Use verbal prompts such as, "Wow, this is a big circle. Can you find another big circle in front of you?" Glue the cutouts onto the place mat as he makes his matches.

Preschooler
Demonstrate how your preschooler can use one hand to hold an object steady and the other hand to trace the object with a crayon. Along with cutting, tracing is a great way to further develop her motor skills.

School-Age Child
After gluing his shapes onto his place mat, your school-age child may enjoy adding colorful food cutouts from a magazine or a supermarket circular. He can depict his favorite meal (like pizza and milk).

Parent Tip
Put these place mats on the table before mealtime. Your older children can use them as a guide to set the table.

Squeeze Me Sponge Art

In this activity, your kids will work with sponges to create wonderful art!

What You'll Need	All Ages	Baby	Toddler	Preschooler	School–Age Child
Child-safe scissors	✋				
New sponges	✋				
Facecloth		✋			
Small baking pans	✋				
Washable tempera paint			✋	✋	✋
Sheets of paper			✋	✋	✋
Stapler				✋	

To get started, you or your school-age child can cut shapes like stars, circles, and squares from new sponges.

Baby

With your baby in her highchair, pour a bit of water into a small baking pan and set it on her tray. Sponges may be a choking hazard, so give her a facecloth to explore instead. If she is six months or older, show her how to dip the facecloth into the water and squeeze it out. This sensation will delight her as she builds her small motor skills and the muscles in her hands. If she is younger than six months, rub the damp cloth on her cheeks. She'll enjoy feeling the new texture.

Toddler

Sponges may be a new art medium for your toddler. Show him how to dip his sponge shape into a baking pan of paint and then press it onto a sheet of paper for a colorful shape collage. This activity is a great chance to review the names of different shapes and colors.

Preschooler

Your preschooler can create a shape-counting book. Label separate sheets of paper "Circle," "Square," and "Triangle" and encourage her to put only the correct sponge shape on the corresponding sheet of paper. This activity aids in word recognition. Once the paint dries, have her count the circles on the circle page and write the number on that page. Do the same for every shape page and then staple the pages together. This will be a great book for her to share with her siblings.

School-Age Child

Your school-age child can create objects or scenes with the sponge shapes. Perhaps he will paint a starry night, using the square and rectangle for a house and the stars for the sky. You can tap into his creative side by suggesting he make abstract art shapes or patterns.

Parent Tip

Have your children help with cleanup. They can wash the table or the baking pans with a clean sponge. Your baby may mimic them by wiping her highchair tray.

Look at Us Now Murals

Using teamwork, your children can create their own life-size body murals.

What You'll Need	All Ages	Baby	Toddler	Preschooler	School-Age Child
Butcher paper (or paper grocery bags taped together)	🖐				
Crayons	🖐				
Tape			🖐		🖐
Mirror				🖐	
Child-safe scissors					🖐

Each child can take a turn lying on a piece of butcher paper while you or your other children trace his or her body with a crayon. There are sure to be some tickle spots along the way!

Baby
It may be difficult for your baby to remain still as her siblings trace around her. Lie her on her belly, side, or back on the butcher paper. Let her move as she wants and trace any pose she makes.

Toddler
Your toddler may prefer standing while you trace him. Tape the paper to the wall and have him stand with his back against it. When the tracing is complete, he will be impressed by his

life-size body outline. Have him identify his body parts by asking, "Where are your legs? Where is your belly?" and so on. As you (or an older sibling) help him add features with crayons, prompt him by asking, "Where should your eyes go?"

Preschooler

If your preschooler helps trace her siblings, encourage her to keep her crayon close to their bodies so her tracings are accurate. When she decorates her own body mural, have her look in the mirror so she can identify which crayons to use to color her hair, eyes, and clothes. She may decide to dress her body mural as a superhero or ballerina.

School-Age Child

Challenge your school-age child to imitate Pablo Picasso, one of the most important artists of the twentieth century. Much of his work involved colorful collages of mismatched objects. For instance, your school-age child can trace a sibling's hand, cut out the tracing, and use it as one of his hands in his body mural. He can also color his features in mismatching colors.

Parent Tip
You may decide to hang the murals together on the wall for a life-size family portrait or individually on your children's bedroom doors as cool decorations.

Portable Seas

Create a mesmerizing, portable sea using water bottles, trinkets, and a little imagination.

What You'll Need	All Ages	Baby	Toddler	Preschooler	School-Age Child
Clear plastic water bottles, ¾ full, with caps	🖐				
Blue food coloring	🖐				
Red and yellow food coloring					🖐
Glue	🖐				
1 teaspoon vegetable oil per bottle					🖐
"Sea objects," like hermit crabs (acorns or rocks), minnows (twisted strips of aluminum foil), sea floor rocks (pebbles), fish (sequins), and dolphins (pieces of drinking straws)	🖐				

Begin by removing the bottle labels and adding a few drops of blue food coloring to the water with your older children's help. While your preschooler and school-age child add "sea objects" to their bottles, your younger children can watch as you add objects to theirs. When the portable seas are completed, use glue to secure the caps to the bottles.

Baby

Your baby will enjoy watching you drop objects into her portable sea. When you're done, place the bottle in front of her on the floor and gently push it so it rolls away. If she is six months or older, this action may entice her to retrieve it. If your baby is younger than six months, hold the bottle close to her ear and tilt it gently back and forth to create waves. The sound may remind her of the womb. To visually stimulate her, hold the bottle in front of her and encourage her to watch the sea objects float back and forth.

Toddler

Let your toddler point to the objects he wants you to add to his bottle. As you drop each one into the water, playfully say, "We're going to pretend this is a hermit crab." Talk about the sea with your toddler. Ask, "Who lives in the sea? How do they get around?" When you're done, he will love using his hands to shake the bottle as hard as he can.

Preschool

Your preschooler will enjoy watching the food coloring mix with the water, and he'll have fun shaking up his sea after he's added his objects. This activity can also be calming once the shaking stops. He may become entranced as he watches the objects slowly settle in the bottle.

School-Age Child

Your school-age child may want a blue sea, but as a variation, give her food coloring in all three primary colors at the beginning of the activity. Ask her to drip two colors into her water bottle and have her predict what color they will create. For instance, blue and red creates purple. Before she chooses her sea objects, ask her to predict which will float and which will sink. Were her predictions correct? She can also add a teaspoon of vegetable oil to her bottle. The oil will float to the top, giving her portable sea the look of a lava lamp.

Parent Tip
The portable sea is a great toy during bath time, car rides, or walks in the stroller.

Wild Wheel of Color

Finger paints offer a chance for your kids to use their favorite art accessories—their hands! In this activity, your children will learn how colors mix together to create new ones.

What You'll Need	All Ages	Baby	Toddler	Preschooler	School-Age Child
Paper plates	🖐				
Pencil	🖐				
Finger paints in primary colors	🖐				
Paper	🖐				
Smocks (or old T-shirt)			🖐	🖐	🖐
Wet wipes	🖐				
Newspaper	🖐				
Plain yogurt		🖐			
Food coloring		🖐			
Wax paper		🖐			

On each paper plate, draw six wedges of equal size, as though slicing a pizza. On every other wedge, dab a bit of finger paint in this color order: red, blue, yellow. Instruct your toddler, preschooler, and school-age child to dip their fingers in the red and blue paint and mix the two together in the blank space between those two colors on their paper plates. Have them do the same for the spaces between the blue and yellow wedges and the yellow and red wedges. When done, they will have a color wheel with red, purple, blue, green, yellow, and orange. Use the wheels to make finger paint creations on a separate sheet of paper.

Note: This activity may be messy, so put smocks or old T-shirts on your children beforehand and have plenty of wet wipes handy to clean up messy fingers when you're done. It's also a good idea to lay newspaper under each child's sheet of paper.

Baby

Babies love to explore with their hands and mouths, so if your baby's eating dairy, make a batch of yogurt "paint" she can enjoy while her siblings enjoy their finger paint. Mix plain yogurt with food coloring and place it on a piece of wax paper on her highchair tray. If your baby is younger than six months, help her develop visual convergence (her two eyes working together) by moving a dried color wheel in front of her from side to side and then from up to down. This activity will strengthen her tracking skills.

Toddler

Your toddler will likely approach this project with enthusiasm! If he fills up his entire page with finger paint art, take a pencil and draw some shapes on the wet paint. Tell him what you are drawing: "Here's a circle. Now, I'll draw a square." Your child may want to try tracing the shapes with his finger. This is a great way to practice his drawing skills.

Preschooler

Your preschooler may enjoy creating patterns with his finger paint. He can create a row of green thumbprints, then a row of blue thumbprints, and so on. Let him take the lead when creating his artwork.

School-Age Child

Have your school-age child create bugs with her finger paints. To create a ladybug, she can use her thumb to press red paint onto the paper and then make purple dots, using her index finger. To create a green caterpillar, she can make a line of green dots.

> At first my two-year-old son didn't like the feel of the squishy paint on his hands. I guess it was a texture thing. The good news is, it didn't take long for finger painting to become an all-time favorite art exploration.
>
> —Lisa

A Village to Call Our Own

This village of recycled milk cartons is fun to create, design, and play with.

What You'll Need	All Ages	Baby	Toddler	Preschooler	School-Age Child
Empty milk cartons and small rocks	🖐				
Masking tape	🖐				
Construction paper	🖐				
Stickers			🖐	🖐	🖐
Child-safe scissors	🖐				
Markers			🖐	🖐	🖐
Glue sticks			🖐	🖐	🖐
Picture of a building					🖐

Wash out empty milk cartons, then cut off the top of each. Place a small rock inside each carton to keep it steady. Using masking tape, cover the cartons with construction paper with your preschooler's and school-age child's help. Then your children can decorate their carton buildings with stickers, paper cutouts, or markers to create windows, doors, and other features. When the carton buildings are finished, the resulting village may include a home, a school, and other favorite places.

Baby

While your older children are busy with their cartons, decorate one for your baby using brightly colored cutouts like a red circle, blue triangle, and yellow square. Place the carton in front of her so she can easily view and touch it. If your baby is older than six months, let her get a close-up view of her siblings' carton buildings (without letting her topple the village). She may crawl, roll, or pull herself to get a closer look.

Toddler
Give your toddler a milk carton that is already wrapped with construction paper. He will have fun decorating his structure with stickers. You can also give him a few paper shape cutouts to glue onto his structure. Name the shapes as you assist him with the glue.

Preschooler
To help your preschooler make his building, have him lay the carton on its side on a sheet of construction paper and use large pieces of masking tape to tape the paper to the carton. Let him use his imagination to create a haunted house, a castle, a library, or whatever he desires. Ask him what his building should look like: "Does it need a door? Some windows?"

School-Age Child
Your school-age child may want to design her own building or work from a picture of a building she wishes to re-create. An image will serve as her guide for window placement, exterior color, and so on.

Muddy Day at the Farm

Your kids can add edible "mud" to their art projects to create the perfect barnyard scenes!

What You'll Need	All Ages	Baby	Toddler	Preschooler	School-Age Child
Prepared chocolate pudding	✋				
Plastic containers			✋	✋	✋
Plastic tablecloth or newspaper			✋	✋	✋
Large zip-close plastic bag		✋			
Farm animal stickers			✋		
Construction paper			✋	✋	✋
Crayons				✋	✋

Give small plastic containers of "mud" (chocolate pudding) to your toddler, preschooler, and school-age child. We recommend covering the workspace with a plastic tablecloth or newspaper. This activity can get messy!

Baby

Place mud in a large zip-close plastic bag for your baby. If your baby is older than six months, let him squeeze it with his hands for a great sensory experience. Be sure to supervise him closely. If your baby is younger than six months, sing a song to salute

animals that love to roll around in mud (and squeeze a new
toe for every "little piggy"):

This little piggy went to the market.
This little piggy stayed home.
This little piggy ate roast beef.
This little piggy had none.
This little piggy went "wee, wee, wee" all the way home.

Toddler

Most toddlers love to get messy, and this activity gives your
toddler the perfect chance to do so. She can place some animal
stickers on her construction paper and use her hands to cover
them in mud!

Preschooler

We know pigs love mud—show your preschooler how to draw
one, using shapes: Have him draw one large circle for the head
and a smaller circle in the center for the snout. Then have him
make small circle eyes and triangles on top of the large circle
for ears. Lastly, he can cover his pig with mud!

School-Age Child

Your school-age child may enjoy designing a barn on her paper
before adding the farm animal stickers and the mud. Let her
get creative with the mud by making a muddy swamp, a
muddy trail, or a mud pile.

Icy Shapes

To keep your family entertained on a cold day or cool on a hot one, make ice they can build with!

What You'll Need	All Ages	Baby	Toddler	Preschooler	School-Age Child
Plastic containers in various shapes and sizes (pie pans, ice cube trays, bowls, etc.)	🖐				
Food coloring	🖐				
Small toys or cereal			🖐	🖐	🖐
Baking sheets			🖐	🖐	🖐
Sponges				🖐	🖐

Fill the containers with water and add a few drops of food coloring into each. If you like, drop small toys (for your older children) or cereal (for your toddler) in the water. Freeze the containers overnight. The next day, pop the shapes out of the containers and onto baking sheets. Then let the fun begin! What can your children build? Is it hard to hold the ice? How does it feel?

Baby

If your baby is older than six months, let her play with a piece of ice on her highchair tray. Make sure the ice is small enough for her to handle but large enough that she can't put it in her mouth. Also make sure it's not a piece with a toy or some cereal in it. As she tries to reach for the ice, it may slip away. If she does grab it, how quickly does she sense the cold? Watch closely as the ice melts, and take it away when it's small enough to put in her mouth. If she is younger than six months, run the ice along her toes for a second. There are thousands of nerve endings on her feet, and she will have a lot of sensation there!

Toddler
Your toddler may enjoy stacking ice cubes or sliding them up and down the baking sheet as they begin to melt. She may be less disappointed when the ice melts if you give her a piece with a cereal surprise inside!

Preschooler
Your preschooler will enjoy building with the ice pieces. To make the frozen shapes stick together, tell your preschooler to use a sponge to dab water onto his ice, then hold the pieces together until they are firmly attached.

School-Age Child
Your school-age child may want to build with the ice, or he may turn it into a hands-on learning experiment. Make some predictions with him. How long will each shape take to melt? Heat will melt them—what else will?

Marvelous Marble Roll

With this art project, your kids will wiggle and move to make a marble create fabulous designs!

What You'll Need	All Ages	Baby	Toddler	Preschooler	School-Age Child
Plastic container with cover			👋		
Shoebox with lid				👋	
Large cardboard box					👋
Paper	👋				
Washable tempera paint	👋				
Marbles (or small balls)	👋				
Wet wipes		👋			
Tennis ball					👋

Find a few containers for your children, like a clear plastic container with a cover for your toddler, a shoebox with a lid for your preschooler, and a large cardboard box for your school-age child. (*Note:* You can keep this activity simple by having all of your children use similar containers.) Place a sheet of paper on the bottom of each container. Add a few dabs of paint to the paper, then drop a marble in each container. Your children can shake and dip their containers from side to side so their marbles roll and make cool designs.

Baby

Lay your baby on a blanket and get her ready to make a special marble design. Dab some paint on a marble and gently roll the marble around the sole of her foot, making any design you choose. She will find the sensation on her feet exhilarating. Press her foot onto paper, and her artwork is complete. Have wet wipes on hand so you can clean her feet as soon as the activity is done.

Toddler

Teach your toddler what happens when she combines two colors in her container. Place a dab of red paint and a dab of blue on the paper, put the marble in her container, and secure the cover. Encourage her to roll the marble around for a few minutes. When she opens the container, what color does she see?

Preschooler

Your preschooler may enjoy leaving off his shoebox's lid and trying to direct the marble across the paper as he dips the box from side to side. Or he may want to put the lid on so the marble's designs will be a surprise when he's finished.

School-Age Child

Work as a team with your school-age child. You can hold one end of a large box and he can hold the other. Then work together to dip the box from side to side. Make a fun game by not letting the marble touch the sides of the box! If you like, try this game with a tennis ball instead of a marble.

Fruity Tie-Dye Shirts

Your kids can create one-of-a-kind T-shirts using this
centuries-old craft. Wear them during a family outing—your
kids will be easy to spot!

What You'll Need	All Ages	Baby	Toddler	Preschooler	School-Age Child
Plain light-colored cotton T-shirts	🖐				
Rubber bands or string	🖐				
Fabric makers		🖐			
Plain light-colored cotton onesie		🖐			
Spray bottle filled with water	🖐				
Large plastic trash bags	🖐				
Large pot	🖐				
Package of fruit drink mix (like Kool-Aid)	🖐				
Spoon	🖐				
Tongs	🖐				
Iron	🖐				

Baby

Using a T-shirt, make a buddy for your baby. Wrap some rubber bands lengthwise around a crumpled T-shirt to create a
caterpillar. Use fabric markers to make some eyes and a smiling mouth. While the other children work with their T-shirts,

start at your baby's feet and wiggle the caterpillar slowly up her body while singing this song:

The itsy-bitsy caterpillar crawled up the baby's leg.
   (Crawl the caterpillar up your baby's leg.)
Wiggled the baby's tummy,
   (Touch her tummy with the caterpillar.)
and jumped up to her head.
   (Place the caterpillar on her head.)
Down came bug and kissed her on the face.
   (Kiss baby with the caterpillar.)
And the itsy-bitsy caterpillar left without a trace.
   (Hide the caterpillar behind your back.)

Toddler, Preschooler, and School-Age Child

Have your toddler, preschooler, and school-age child dunk their T-shirts—plus a onesie for the baby—in the tub or spray them with water. Make sure the shirts are completely wet. Lay a plastic bag on the ground for each child to serve as a work space. Have your children crumple, fold, and twist the shirts to make them as small as possible. (Your toddler may need assistance.) Then work together to bind the shirts tightly with rubber bands or string. To create the dye, make the fruit drink in a large pot. For four shirts, make four servings. For two shirts, make two servings. Your kids can help stir.

While the kids watch from a safe distance, boil the fruit drink, then cool it to room temperature. Place the shirts in the mixture and let them soak for twenty minutes. To make the wait go faster for your kids, ask them to predict what the shirts will look like when they're done or have them sing the "Itsy-Bitsy Caterpillar" song to the baby. You could also play a few activities from the Out & About Chapter, like "Freeze!" (page 166) and "Ten Things" (page 178).

After the shirts have soaked, remove them from the pot using tongs. Your children will enjoy their fruity scent. Pull a chair up to the sink so your older kids can take turns watching you run cold water over each shirt, or do this step outside with the hose. They can tell you when the water runs clear. Remove the rubber bands and rinse the shirts again. Your kids can help hang the shirts to dry. Iron them if necessary once dry, then wear them!

Colorful Collages

Enjoy some colorful drawings by creating a collage of images.

What You'll Need	All Ages	Baby	Toddler	Preschooler	School-Age Child
Crayons			🖐	🖐	🖐
Coloring books				🖐	🖐
White construction paper			🖐		
Colorful blankets or pillow cases		🖐			
Towels		🖐			
Child-safe scissors			🖐	🖐	🖐
Glue sticks			🖐	🖐	🖐
Poster board			🖐	🖐	🖐

To begin this activity, your preschooler and school-age child can color some pages from favorite coloring books, and your toddler can color on white construction paper. They'll then use these colorful images to design collages.

Baby

While your older children work on their collages, you can create a blanket collage for your baby to explore. Layer and angle three to four different colored blankets or pillow cases on the floor. Make a bolster by rolling a few towels together lengthwise, then place the baby on her tummy over the bolster so she has a great view of the collage. Looking at colorful patterns

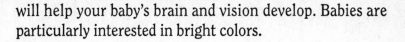

will help your baby's brain and vision develop. Babies are particularly interested in bright colors.

Toddler

Cut out several shapes from the white construction paper your toddler colored as well as from other sheets of construction paper. Ask her to identify the shapes and colors. With your help, she can glue them onto poster board.

Preschooler

At this age, many preschoolers can begin to use a pair of child-safe scissors. This activity is a great way to help your preschooler develop this skill. Tear out the pages he has colored from his coloring book. Make sure they feature fairly large images for him to cut out. Then he can glue the images onto poster board.

School-Age Child

When your school-age child finishes cutting out images from the coloring books, encourage him to arrange the drawings in a fun pattern—upside down or even overlapping—before he glues the images in place on poster board. He may even want to use crayons to create a backdrop or scene for his collage.

> On his bedroom walls, my son proudly displays collages he has created from old coloring books.
>
> —Lisa

King and Queen Crowns

Who wouldn't enjoy being king or queen for the day?
Everyone can enjoy the prestige that comes with these
easy-to-make crowns!

What You'll Need	All Ages	Baby	Toddler	Preschooler	School-Age Child
Child-safe scissors	✋				
Construction paper in various colors	✋				
Art supplies, such as crayons, stickers, stamps, cotton balls, aluminum foil, and so on	✋				
Tape	✋				
Glue	✋				
Paper plates		✋			✋
Glitter					✋

For each crown, cut a sheet of construction paper into two
strips lengthwise—one strip 2 inches wide and the other about
6 inches wide. Let your children decorate the 6-inch strips
with a variety of art supplies. When they've finished, tape the
two strips together in a circle, adjusting the narrower strip to
fit the circumference of the child's head.

Baby

While your older children create their crowns, you can introduce your baby to different textures. Simply glue a few of the

crown materials (such a cotton ball, foil, and some tape) to a paper plate. Place his hand on each item and tell him what he is touching. Provide one-word descriptions such as "soft," "crunchy" and "smooth." Also have his siblings make and decorate a crown for him. Perhaps your school-age child can write a term of endearment on it such as, "Our Little Prince!"

Toddler
Your toddler can decorate his crown with stickers, crayons, and stamps. To create jewels, cut diamond shapes from construction paper and help him glue them onto his crown. He can also add cotton balls or pieces of foil to his dazzling headpiece. Write his name on the crown.

Preschooler
Your preschooler may want to cut her own construction paper strips for her crown, which is a great opportunity to work on her scissor skills. To help her, fold her construction paper at the 2-inch mark and let her follow the crease with her scissors. If she desires, she can cut a pattern along the top of the 6-inch strip to add a design to her crown.

School-Age Child
Your school-age child's crown can sparkle with a bit of glitter. Have her put glue on her crown and sprinkle glitter over the glue. Have her tip the crown and gently tap the excess glitter onto a paper plate. Allow the glue to dry.

Parent Tip
To get into the spirit, address your children as "King"
or "Queen" when they wear their crowns. This is a great
photo opportunity!

Goobly-Goop

This fun, goopy substance changes from solid to liquid with a touch of your hand.

What You'll Need	All Ages	Baby	Toddler	Preschooler	School-Age Child
½ cup cornstarch	🖐				
¼ cup water	🖐				
Food coloring	🖐				
Pie pans	🖐				
Zip-close plastic bag		🖐			
Plastic spoon and cups			🖐		
Small plastic toys				🖐	
Seashell or rock collection				🖐	

To make goobly-goop, mix the first three ingredients in a pie pan for each child. Your older children may want to help, especially with the food coloring. The finished substance will thrill your children: Upon first touch, it feels solid, but it quickly turns to liquid when tiny fingers touch it, generating heat.

Baby

If your baby is younger than six months, lay him on his back and let him kick a clean pie pan with his feet while his siblings play with the goop. He'll like the metallic bang he can create.

If your baby is older, place his portion of the goobly-goop in a zip-close plastic bag. Let him squeeze and pat the bag.

Toddler
At the beginning of the activity, let your toddler decide what color he'd like you to make his goobly-goop. Once the substance is ready, he can discover different ways to handle it, using tools such as a spoon and cups. For example, he may decide to transfer the goop from cup to cup with the spoon.

Preschooler
As you prepare the goobly-goop, have your preschooler add her own food coloring to create the perfect shade. After exploring the goop with her hands, encourage her to play with small plastic toys in the goop. It can make toy car tracks disappear or, if thick enough, hold a figurine in place.

School-Age Child
To thicken the consistency, have your school-age child add more cornstarch to her goop. Thicker goop will hold things in place and may be perfect for arranging a seashell or rock collection. She can also put some goop in her hand and drip it over a clean pan to write out her name or initials.

Canvas Painting

This activity uses a huge canvas to encourage free artistic expression full of possibilities!

What You'll Need	All Ages	Baby	Toddler	Preschooler	School-Age Child
Old flat sheet	✋				
Clothesline and clothes-pins (or 2 chairs and a rope)	✋				
Washable tempera paint	✋				
Sponge			✋		
Paintbrush				✋	
Spray bottle					✋

The outdoors may be the best place for this activity, but you can do it indoors if you have enough room. If you're outdoors, hang an old sheet on a clothesline, making sure your children can easily reach it. If you're indoors or if don't have a clothesline, set up two chairs and tie a rope between them. Lay the sheet over the rope. Either way, your children will have a blast decorating the "canvas."

Baby

Before the painting begins, sit next to the hanging sheet with your baby. Your older children may even engage in a game of peekaboo with her! Have your baby touch the sheet with her hands and her feet. To encourage artistic expression, put a little paint on her finger and let her smear the sheet. Even though tempera paint is nontoxic, supervise her closely so she doesn't put her finger in her mouth.

Toddler
Your toddler will enjoy decorating the canvas using a sponge dipped in paint. He can blot or smear paint on the sheet.

Preschooler
This activity will challenge your preschooler's motor skills. Encourage him to paint the top part of the canvas with a paintbrush; he'll need to reach above his chest and use the muscles required to write—a great exercise for the future!

School-Age Child
Fill a spray bottle half with paint and half with water. Your school-age child can squirt the sheet to create unique designs.

Parent Tip
Use the finished painting to decorate a playroom or other space in your home.

Stay Still Art

We know kids don't usually stay still for long, but this still life art project will inspire them to stay at rest!

What You'll Need	All Ages	Baby	Toddler	Preschooler	School-Age Child
Still life art (see suggestions below)	✋				
Drawing paper			✋	✋	✋
Crayons			✋	✋	✋
Pencil					✋

Make a still life art setting on the center of your kitchen table. You can use plush animals, a bowl of fruit, a vase with flowers, some colorful mugs, or any household decoration. Pass out paper and crayons and encourage your older children to draw what they see. There is no right or wrong in art, as long as making it is fun!

Baby

Young babies can see bold, contrasting colors, but it will be awhile before they can identify the names of each. In the meantime, introduce your baby to colors through touch, using objects from the still life art setting. For example, rub a flower petal on her cheek and say, "This purple petal is smooth." Gently dip her hand in a glass of cool water and say, "This clear water is cool." Snuggle a teddy bear on your baby's chest, and say, "This brown bear is soft."

Toddler

Help your toddler study the still life setting. He may be particularly interested if it includes an object he is familiar with, like a favorite plush animal. What colors and shapes does he see? He may be able to match a color he sees with a crayon for his drawing.

Preschooler

This activity should be a fun exercise for your preschooler. As she enters the preschool years, her drawings may become more defined with specific shapes and colors. To help her get started, she may prefer that you draw an outline of the setting she can trace over with her crayon. Teach her how to make dark marks by firmly pressing her crayon and light marks by brushing it softly over the paper.

School-Age Child

Encourage your school-age child to take his time studying the objects placed on the table. He can study shapes, contrasts, and textures. Suggest he sketch the setting first, using a pencil. Once he is satisfied with the sketch, he can color in the objects.

Surprise Designs

Your kids will love to see their colorful designs magically reappear in this activity.

What You'll Need	All Ages	Baby	Toddler	Preschooler	School-Age Child
White construction paper	🖐				
Crayons	🖐				
Scissors		🖐			
Paintbrushes			🖐	🖐	🖐
Diluted black tempera paint			🖐	🖐	🖐
Clear plastic water bottles and small colored objects		🖐			
Rubber band			🖐		
White chalk					🖐

Give your older children each a sheet of white construction paper. Encourage them to draw, scribble, and color the entire sheet with crayons. Cut a 1-inch-wide strip from each of their papers for your baby's part of the activity. After cutting the strips, have your children paint diluted black paint all over their papers. As the paint dries, their designs will reveal themselves. The paint is water-based and thus less dense than the crayon markings, allowing the colors to pop through!

Baby

Place the 1-inch strips into a clear plastic water bottle for your baby. Secure the bottle cap tightly and give it to your baby, letting him explore the colors within. You also can create a red bottle, a blue bottle, and a green bottle by placing objects of corresponding colors inside each.

Toddler

Use a rubber band to wrap three crayons together. Your toddler's small hand will have an easier time holding them, and he'll be able to add many colors to his paper instantly. When it's time to add the black paint, he may also appreciate a larger paintbrush that will let him paint broader strokes.

Preschooler

For fun, write your preschooler's name in large bubble letters across the paper. Have her color in the letters with squiggly lines, stripes, or crisscrossed lines. She'll enjoy seeing her name appear when the paint dries.

School-Age Child

Suggest that your school-age child create a maze with crayons. She can start with a large square with an entrance and exit. Then she can create a maze of tunnels to connect the entrance and exit. Have her add some blocked areas as well. Once the paint dries, she or another sibling can use white chalk to complete the maze.

Apple Art

We know apples are good to eat, but they're also good for creating deliciously fun art.

What You'll Need	All Ages	Baby	Toddler	Preschool	School-Age Child
Apples (any variety)	🖐				
Knife	🖐				
Popsicle sticks			🖐	🖐	🖐
Washable tempera paint			🖐	🖐	🖐
Paper plates			🖐	🖐	🖐
Sheets of white paper			🖐	🖐	🖐
Yogurt		🖐			
Butcher paper				🖐	🖐
Crayons				🖐	🖐

Cut the apples vertically in half. With the flat side down, vertically insert a Popsicle stick in the center of the apple. Your children can use these homemade "stamps" to make paintings. Pour paint onto paper plates, then have your children dip the apples into the paint and gently press them onto paper.

Baby

Take your baby's hands and explore an apple half together. Let her smell and touch the fruit. If she is over six months and eating dairy, you can place some yogurt on her highchair tray as edible "paint." Closely supervise her as she swirls the apple around in the yogurt.

Toddler

Show your toddler how to use the stamp by holding the stick, pressing the apple onto the paper, and then lifting it up. Or instead of stamping the page, she may choose to use the apple as a paintbrush. Let her do so!

Preschooler and School-Age Child

Your preschooler and school-age child can create their own apple tree painting. Lay a large sheet of butcher paper on the floor and encourage them to use crayons to draw a tree outline, including branches and leaves. Then they can add apples to the tree by using their apple stamps. How many apples can their tree hold?

Parent Tip

When you're done creating apple art, your preschooler and school-age child can begin the process of planting an apple tree. Put seeds in a paper towel, place them in the refrigerator, and keep the paper towel moist for a week or so. When you notice sprouts, it is time to transfer them to a cup with soil. Place the cup on a sunny windowsill and keep the soil moist. In a week, the sprouts will be ready to be planted outside. Choose a sunny location and continue to water them. With love and care, you will have more apples to eat and use for art! You may even want to plant two sprouts because apple trees grow best in pairs.

Pipe Cleaner Flowers

Your children can bend and twist pipe cleaners to create flowers that will brighten any room!

What You'll Need	All Ages	Baby	Toddler	Preschooler	School-Age Child
Small bell		🖐			
Pipe cleaners	🖐				
Glue	🖐				
Construction paper		🖐	🖐		
Paintbrushes			🖐	🖐	🖐
Washable tempera paint	🖐				
Wax paper				🖐	🖐
String				🖐	🖐

Baby

Attach a small bell to a pipe cleaner and gently secure it to your baby's ankle. Each time she kicks, crawls, or moves her legs, she will hear the bell jingle. She'll love the gentle sound and the soft feel of the pipe cleaner against her skin. For your baby's flower, make a circle with a green pipe cleaner and glue it onto construction paper. Once the glue dries, you can dip her index finger into yellow paint and gently press it around the green circle to create petals.

Toddler

Most toddlers will enjoy the fuzzy feel and flexibility of pipe cleaners. Let your toddler play with her pipe cleaner and bend it into whatever design she chooses. Give her several to twist together, and help her glue them onto construction paper. She can use paint to create pretty flowers to embellish her pipe cleaner design.

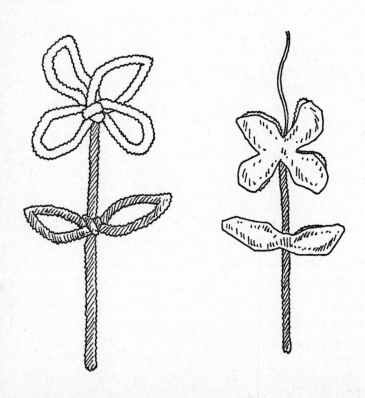

Preschooler and School-Age Child

Show your preschooler and school-age child how to create a flower made from pipe cleaners. *Note:* Most preschoolers will be able to create the circles but may need assistance with other steps.

- **Leaves:** Bend a pipe cleaner into a circle and twist it closed. Then twist the circle in the center, creating a figure eight. Mold into leaf shapes.
- **Petals:** Bend a pipe cleaner into a circle and twist it closed. Then twist the circle in the center, creating a figure eight. Mold into petal shapes. Repeat with another pipe cleaner. Twist the four petals together to create a bloom shape.
- **Stem:** Attach the leaves in the middle of a pipe cleaner and twist the flower to the top.

Lay the design on wax paper and squeeze glue into the empty spaces of the petals and leaves. When it is dry, your children can fill in the petals and leaves with paint. Then help them cut away the excess wax paper, tie string to the pipe cleaner flowers, and hang them by a window.

Spin, Spin Pinwheel

This spinning wheel of color will dazzle your children.

What You'll Need	All Ages	Baby	Toddler	Preschooler	School-Age Child
Scissors	🖐				
Ledger-size printing paper	🖐				
Crayons	🖐				
Stickers	🖐				
Pencil	🖐				
Pin	🖐				
Dowel	🖐				

Note: The materials above will create one pinwheel, but you may decide to have your older children each make their own with your assistance. For each pinwheel, cut ledger paper into a large square. Put it within everyone's reach on a table. Have your children decorate the front and back with crayons and stickers. Your school-age child may want to write the names of each family member on it.

Let your older children assist with the assembly:

1. Fold the paper from opposite corner to opposite corner, and then unfold. Do the same for the other corners.
2. Make a pencil mark on each fold about one-third from the center.

3. Cut along the folds, stopping at the pencil marks.
   This will create eight points.
4. Fold every other point to the center.
5. Stick a pin through all four points in the center.
   The head of the pin will form the hub of the pinwheel.
6. Stick the pin into a thin dowel.
7. Enjoy!

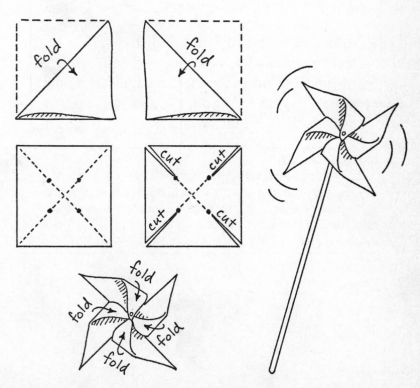

Baby

Babies love to watch colorful, moving objects. Sit with her as you gently blow the pinwheel and let her enjoy the visual display.

Toddler

Teach your toddler how to move the pinwheel by making an O shape with his lips and blowing onto the center of the pinwheel.

Preschooler and School-Age Child

Your preschooler and school-age child may decide to create their own pinwheels with different themes. Before pinning their pinwheels together, they can use crayons to create a patriotic, springtime, or rainbow theme.

> **Did You Know?**
> On the annual International Day of Peace (September 21), people should plant pinwheels outdoors as a public statement of peace. The spinning pinwheels represent the peaceful thoughts and feelings spinning throughout the world!

Faces Fit for a Frame

Use empty CD cases to create easy-to-display picture frames.

What You'll Need	All Ages	Baby	Toddler	Preschooler	School-Age Child
Empty CD cases	🖐				
Child-safe scissors	🖐				
Construction paper	🖐				
Family photos (or photocopies of them)	🖐				
Crayons, stickers, or puzzle pieces	🖐				
Tape or glue sticks	🖐				
Pencil			🖐		🖐

For each case, cut two pieces of construction paper: One to cover the case's inside front cover, and another to cover the CD tray. Help your children select photos of their faces to glue onto one of the pieces, then they can decorate around the photo with crayons or stickers. They'll decorate the second piece of paper according to their age-specific instructions below. When both pieces are finished, use tape or glue to affix one to the inside front cover and the other over the tray.

Baby

Flip through family photos with your baby while the other children work on their projects. Babies love to study friendly faces. Tell her who is in each photo. You or your older children can also create a frame for your baby. Place some photos of her with her siblings as a great keepsake of this activity.

Toddler

Give your toddler some stickers or puzzle pieces to decorate around his photo. (Help him with the glue.) You can also use a pencil to record recent milestones on the other piece of paper. Remember to include the date.

Preschooler

At this age, some preschoolers can draw faces with appropriate features. Have your preschooler choose a photo to glue onto one side of the case, then have him draw a picture of the photo on the second piece. He'll use his developing observational and drawing skills to duplicate features.

School-Age Child

On the second piece of paper, your school-age child can write a narrative about what is happening in the photo she glued onto the other piece. What is she doing in the photo? How is she feeling?

Wild Animal Flashcards

Create your very own flashcards using animal images from magazines and coloring books.

What You'll Need	All Ages	Baby	Toddler	Preschooler	School-Age Child
Old magazines or coloring books	🖐				
Child-safe scissors			🖐	🖐	🖐
Glue sticks			🖐	🖐	🖐
Large index cards			🖐	🖐	🖐
Colored pencils or markers					🖐

You or your older children can begin this activity by finding animal images in magazines or coloring books. They can then cut out and glue the images onto index cards.

Baby

While your older children find or create animal images, your baby will love ripping, tearing, and crinkling the pages of glossy magazines. He'll enjoy seeing the contrasting, bright images and hearing the pages rip. If they like, your older children can flip through the magazines and describe the images to your baby.

Toddler

Your toddler will enjoy finding animal images for her flash-cards. This task will help develop her ability to classify objects. Once she finds an animal, be sure to ask her, "What animal is this?" and "What sound does this animal make?" Help her glue the images onto index cards.

Preschooler

Challenge your preschooler to sort his animal images according to size, habitation (land or sea), and other groupings before gluing them onto the index cards. This is a great way to sharpen his organizational and observational skills. Be sure to ask him, "Which group do you have the most of?" or "What is your favorite animal and why?"

School-Age Child

Encourage your school-age child to strengthen her drawing skills by making symmetry art. Have her cut an animal image in half and glue one half onto an index card. Challenge her to draw the other half of the image, using colored pencils or markers.

Recyclables

With imagination, your children can create cars, figurines, or their own inventions using recyclable materials.

What You'll Need	All Ages	Baby	Toddler	Preschooler	School-Age Child
Recyclable materials (including toilet paper or paper towel tubes, egg cartons, aluminum foil, Popsicle sticks, plastic cups, tissue paper, and so on)	✋				
Grocery bags			✋	✋	✋
Art supplies (including crayons, construction paper, masking tape, wax paper, pipe cleaners, and pompoms)			✋	✋	✋
Contact paper		✋			✋

Place various recyclable items into separate grocery bags for your toddler, preschooler, and school-age child. As your children pull out the objects, they'll be busy imagining the different ways they can use each object. Also provide them with art supplies to help them turn the recyclables into whatever their imaginations desire. This activity requires lots of artistic expression and creativity.

Baby

Tape a small piece of contact paper sticky side up in front of your baby. Slowly stick a toilet paper tube to the paper, then peel it off. If she is six months or older, encourage her to stick and peel off the tube herself. By eight months, most babies can solve simple problems like getting an object by pulling it. No matter her age, she'll enjoy the tearing sound.

Toddler

Your toddler will love to sort and explore the objects in her bag. If possible, make sure to put an egg carton in it. She'll love this wonderful organizer. For example, she can use it to sort pompoms according to color. Or she may choose to use the carton for a different activity, here's how: Flip the egg carton over and poke Popsicle sticks through the bottom of each cup. She'll have fun moving them in and out.

Preschooler

Your preschooler will enjoy finding new uses for the recyclables, such as making his own pencil holder from a large plastic cup and some masking tape. Have him use small strips of masking tape to completely cover the cup in layered designs.

School-Age Child

Your school-age child may decide to create a three-dimensional scene by sticking his objects to contact paper. Ideas include a playground (he can cut a toilet paper tube in half lengthwise to create a slide or use Popsicle sticks to create monkey bars) or a garden (he can make a colorful flower patch with colored tissue paper). A decorated sheet of construction paper can serve as the backdrop to any scene. Simply have him make a stiff crease one inch from one side of the construction paper and attach the fold to the contact paper.

> My son loved making inventions with recyclable materials. The most memorable one was a "candy maker." He explained to me in detail how the contraption works, and he worked on it for over an hour!
>
> —Heather

Let Our Feet Do the Painting

Your children will love using their feet to create art in this activity.

What You'll Need	All Ages	Baby	Toddler	Preschooler	School-Age Child
Newspaper	✋				
Tape	✋				
Sheets of plain art paper	✋				
Washable tempera paint	✋				
2–4 large, flat pans	✋				
Medium-size paintbrushes	✋				
Wet wipes	✋				
Toy cars or plastic dinosaurs				✋	✋

Dress your children in old clothes; shorts may be best. Spread newspaper on the floor, then tape enough plain art paper onto the newspaper to create a 4-by-8-foot walking space for each child. Pour paint into two large, flat pans and then have your kids remove their shoes and socks. Before you paint their feet, make sure the children know they must stay on the art paper and newspaper until you clean their feet with wet wipes at the end of the project!

Baby

Your baby will enjoy the sensation of the cool, wet paint on the soles of his tiny feet. If your baby is younger than six months, have him sit on your lap as you kneel next to the paper. Gently press his painted feet onto the paper. If he's older than six months, help him "walk" across the paper. This activity is a perfect way to capture some of his first steps.

Toddler

Your toddler may want to help paint the soles of her siblings' feet. She'll love to have her feet painted, too, and she'll enjoy walking across the paper. Encourage her to tiptoe or slide.

Preschooler and School-Age Child

Encourage your older children to create dance patterns or other creative designs with their feet. To make some crazy tracks, they can dip their toy cars' wheels or plastic dinosaurs' feet into the paint and roll or walk them across the paper.

Very Cool Fruity Play Dough

This play dough has a yummy and fruity scent! Plus, it's safe to taste!

What You'll Need	All Ages	Baby	Toddler	Preschooler	School age
Homemade play dough (see recipe on next page)	✋				
Wax paper	✋				
Kitchen gadgets				✋	✋
Child-safe scissors				✋	✋
Tree leaves				✋	✋

Your preschooler and school-age child can help you prepare the play dough. When it has cooled, they can divide it evenly among the siblings. The children will love the fun, fruity scent. Have each child put wax paper down on his or her workspace.

Baby

If your baby is younger than six months, hold some play dough close her nose so she can smell the fruity aroma. If she's older, let her explore a small amount under your supervision.

Toddler

Your toddler may choose to bang, pound, and roll his play dough into various shapes and sizes. Show him how to flatten the dough and press his hand in it to create a handprint.

Preschooler and School-Age Child

Here are some ways your preschooler and school-age child can have fun with their play dough:

- Make cookies: Use kitchen gadgets to roll out the dough and cut out cookie shapes.
- Practice using scissors: This dough slices easily and grips the child-safe scissors better than paper does.
- Create leaf imprints: Flatten the dough and press leaves into it.
- Make figurines: Design clowns, cars, and other objects.

Play Dough Recipe

½ cup salt
2 cups water
Fruit drink mix (like Kool-Aid)
2 tablespoons vegetable oil
2 cups sifted flour
2 tablespoons alum

Combine salt and water in saucepan and boil until the salt dissolves. Remove from heat and tint with fruit drink mix. Add oil, flour, and alum. Knead until smooth. This dough will last two months in an airtight container or zip-close freezer bag.

CHAPTER 10
In the Kitchen

Your kitchen is the hub of your home. It's where you connect as a family at the dinner table. Our kids love to put on their mini aprons and whip up some snacks or crack some eggs for our special scrambled eggs. Sure, they have fun making the meals, but they have even more fun tasting the results of their hard work!

—Heather and Lisa

Kitchen activities are a great way to spend time together as a family. They require teamwork and help develop your children's hand-eye coordination, math and reading skills, and small motor skills. Plus, they produce tasty creations your whole family can enjoy!

The recipes in this chapter provide tasty and easy things our children have enjoyed making with us. While the process of following the recipe was fun for our kids, they especially loved eating the product. They're beginning to realize that no meal is quite so delicious as one they help make!

Children of all ages can help prepare these recipes. After choosing a recipe, read it through with your children and explain any unknown words. Gather the necessary ingredients and supplies. In each recipe, we suggest specific ways toddlers, preschoolers, and school-age children can help, and below you'll find additional ideas for how your "assistant chefs" can help prepare any recipe with your supervision:

Baby

- Watch all the action from her highchair or bouncy seat.
- Smell the food as it cooks.
- Play with a clean, easy-to-hold food item like an apple or potato or play with measuring cups.
- "Supervise" her fellow assistant chefs.

Toddler

- Pour and mix premeasured dry ingredients.
- Spread butter, margarine, peanut butter, and other spreads.
- Roll dough into balls.
- Grease pans with fingers.

Preschooler

- Wash fruits and vegetables.
- Measure dry ingredients.
- Arrange items on a baking sheet.
- Crack eggs.

School-Age Child

- Peel vegetables.
- Slice fruits and vegetables.
- Measure liquid ingredients.
- Use the mixer.

Although the kitchen is certainly an exciting environment, it's also a hazardous one for unsupervised children. Always keep dangerous objects out of your children's reach and closely supervise children using sharp utensils or hot appliances. In fact, until you're certain of a child's abilities, make it a rule that only an adult can handle these items. Make sure to also emphasize healthy habits like washing hands before handling food and after handling potentially harmful foods (like raw eggs).

Five-Minute Scrambled Eggs

Your kids will scramble to help make these delicious eggs!

4 eggs
4 tablespoons milk
4 tablespoons cottage cheese or shredded cheese
1 cup chopped green pepper, spinach, or other vegetable

1. Crack the eggs and pour the contents into a bowl. Your preschooler can do this task. Make sure he washes his hands thoroughly after handling the eggs.
2. Beat the eggs with a fork until the liquid is yellow.
3. Stir in the milk, cheese, and vegetables. Your school-age child can measure these ingredients and add them to the beaten eggs, and your toddler can help you stir the contents.
4. Spray a pan with cooking spray, then heat the pan over medium heat.
5. Cook the egg mixture, stirring occasionally until firm, about 5 minutes. This recipe makes 4 servings.

My sisters and I loved making these eggs as kids. In fact, we coined the name Five-Minute Scrambled Eggs because we worked as a team and had our breakfast on the table in no time at all!

—Heather

Mac & Cheese

This recipe is from Trish Kuffner's *The Children's Busy Book* (Meadowbrook Press), and it's one of our family's favorites! We've adapted it so all your kids can help prepare it.

2 cups uncooked macaroni
2 tablespoons butter
1 small onion, minced (optional)
1 tablespoon all-purpose flour
1 teaspoon salt
¼ teaspoon dry mustard
Dash of pepper
1½ cups milk
2 cups shredded Cheddar

1. Preheat your oven to 350°F. Cook and drain the macaroni according to package instructions, then set it aside in a bowl.
2. Your toddler can grease a 2-quart casserole dish. Unwrap one end of a stick of butter and have her rub it all over the bottom and sides of the dish.
3. Melt 2 tablespoons butter in a saucepan over medium heat. If you like, add the onion and sauté it until tender.
4. Combine the flour, salt, mustard, and pepper in a small bowl. Your preschooler can do this task. Stir the mixture into the butter, then slowly stir in the milk.

5. Cook the mixture, stirring constantly, until it's smooth and slightly thickened.
6. Remove the saucepan from the heat. Add cheese and stir until it melts.
7. Put the cooked macaroni in the casserole dish and pour the cheese mixture over the macaroni. Your school-age child can do this step.
8. Bake the macaroni until it's bubbly, about 20 minutes. This recipe makes 4 servings as a main dish or 6 servings as a side dish.

Taco Volcano

This twist on a Mexican favorite may encourage your children to try new foods!

1 package large soft tortillas *Sliced avocado*
1 pound lean ground beef *Mild salsa*
1 package taco seasoning *Sour cream*
1 can refried beans *Grated cheese*

1. Cook the beef over medium-high heat until it's no longer pink. Drain the fat, then mix in the taco seasoning according to package instructions.
2. Place the beef, refried beans, avocado, salsa, sour cream, and cheese in individual bowls on the table.
3. Have your children each lay a tortilla on a plate and spoon a small mound of refried beans on it to make a mountain.
4. Your children can then place avocado slices around the edge of the tortilla to make grass. They can spoon beef around the refried beans to create a rocky landscape around the mountain.
5. To turn the mountain into a volcano, the children can top the refried beans with salsa, sour cream, and cheese to create lava and ash.
6. To eat the taco volcano, roll it up and enjoy!

Pizza Faces

Personal-size pizzas get some personality with this fun recipe!

Pizza sauce
English muffins (one half per child)
Toppings, like bell pepper strips, olives and cherry
  tomatoes (cut in half), mushroom slices, ham
  slices, and pineapple pieces
Shredded cheese

1. Preheat your oven to 350°F.
2. Use a spoon to spread pizza sauce on half of an English muffin. Your preschooler and school-age child can do this step, and your toddler can do it with your help.
3. Arrange the toppings to make a face on the muffin. Encourage your children to use toppings they don't regularly eat. Even picky eaters will want to eat their personal creations! Top with shredded cheese and place on a baking sheet.
4. Bake the pizzas for 10 minutes or until cheese is melted.

Fruity Pastry Cups

Your kids will love to make these pastry cups as much as they'll love eating them!

Vegetable oil
9-inch refrigerated pie crust, thawed (for example,
  Pillsbury Refrigerated Pie Crust)
8-ounce tub of cottage cheese
Fruit toppings, such as diced strawberries, apples,
  pineapples, or bananas

1. Preheat your oven to 450°F.
2. Lightly grease a muffin pan with vegetable oil. This is a good task for your toddler.
3. Roll the pie crust out on a piece of wax paper. Press a plastic cup (about 5 inches in diameter) upside down onto the pie crust to cut circles. You should be able to make 8–10 circles. Your children can help with this step.
4. Gently pull the crust with your hands to stretch each circle a bit. Press each circle into a cup so the crust resembles a muffin cup liner. This is a good task for your preschooler.
5. Bake for 6 minutes or until golden.
6. After the pastries have cooled for at least 10 minutes, your school-age child can fill each cup three-quarters full with cottage cheese.
7. Your children can top the cottage cheese with their choice of fruit.

Oatmeal Pancakes

Here's another family favorite adapted from Trish Kuffner's *The Children's Busy Book* (Meadowbrook Press).

½ cup all-purpose flour
½ cup quick-cooking oats
¾ cup buttermilk
¼ cup milk
1 tablespoon sugar
2 tablespoons vegetable oil

1 teaspoon baking powder
½ teaspoon baking soda
½ teaspoon salt
1 egg
Toppings, such as butter and
   syrup, applesauce, or jam

1. Pour all the ingredients except the toppings into a large bowl. Your preschooler can add the liquid ingredients, and your toddler can add the dry ingredients.
2. Beat the ingredients until the batter is smooth. Your children can take turns doing this step.
3. For each pancake, pour ¼ cup of batter onto a hot nonstick griddle or frying pan. Your school-age child can help with this step.
4. Fry the pancakes until they bubble and their edges are dry. Flip the pancakes and cook the other sides until they're golden brown.
5. Serve the pancakes with toppings. This recipe makes 10–12 pancakes.

Tasty Banana Bread

This banana bread is a healthy afternoon snack or bedtime treat.

4 ripe bananas
⅓ cup butter, melted
¾–1 cup sugar
1 egg, beaten

1 teaspoon vanilla
1 teaspoon baking soda
Pinch of salt
1½ cup all-purpose flour

1. Preheat your oven to 350°F.
2. Your toddler can grease a 4-by-8-inch loaf pan. Unwrap one end of a stick of butter and have him rub it all over the bottom and sides of the pan.
3. Have your children peel the bananas then mash them with forks, spoons, or even their hands. They can each mash a banana in a small bowl, then dump the mashed banana into a large mixing bowl.
4. Add the melted butter to the bananas and mix with a wooden spoon. Then mix in the sugar, egg, and vanilla. Your preschooler can do this step.
5. Sprinkle the baking soda and salt over the mixture, then mix them in. Stir in the flour. Your school-age child can do this step.
6. Pour the batter into the loaf pan and bake for 1 hour. Cool on a rack.

Toasted Banana Treat

Your little monkeys will love making this banana treat!

Bread slices (one per child)
Ripe bananas (one per child)
Ground cinnamon

1. Preheat your oven to 450°F.
2. Use your fist to pound the bread slices until they're flattened. Your children will love doing this step! Place the pounded bread onto a baking sheet.
3. Slice the bananas. Your school-age child can do this task with a butter knife. Your preschooler can even do it with a spoon.
4. Place the slices on the bread. Your preschooler and school-age child may want to arrange the slices in a design.
5. Sprinkle cinnamon on the banana slices. Your toddler can help with this task.
6. Bake the bread for 10 minutes or until it's toasted to a light brown.

Parent Tip
Instead of bananas and cinnamon, try strawberries and honey or blueberries and cream cheese.

Fragrant Cinnamon Buns

These delicious cinnamon buns will delight your kids' senses!

2 cups biscuit mix (for example, Bisquick)
⅔ cup milk
Flour
Margarine
¼ cup sugar
1 teaspoon ground cinnamon

1. Preheat your oven to 425°F. Your toddler can grease the baking sheet. Unwrap one end of a stick of butter and have him rub it all over the bottom and sides of the sheet.
2. In a small bowl, combine the biscuit mix with the milk until it forms a dough.
3. Gently knead the dough on a floured surface. Your school-age child will enjoy this step.
4. Roll the dough into an 8-by-12-inch rectangle and spread margarine to cover it completely. This is a good task for your preschooler.
5. In another small bowl, mix the sugar with the cinnamon. Your toddler can do this task. Then sprinkle the mixture on the dough to cover it completely.

6. Roll the dough tightly from one short end to the other, then pinch the ends closed. Your school-age child can do this step.
7. Cut the rolled dough at 1-inch intervals to make circles, then place them on the greased baking sheet.
8. Bake the dough for 15 minutes. This recipe makes 6 buns.

Parent Tip
Cinnamon buns can be stored in your refrigerator for 2–3 weeks and in your freezer for up to 3 months.

Homemade Butter

Let your kids move, shake, and wiggle as they make this butter.

1 pint heavy whipping cream
Salt (optional)

1. Pour the cream into a clean 32-ounce jar (a mayonnaise jar works great).
2. Wrap the jar in a dishtowel and secure with a rubber band to prevent the jar from breaking if dropped.
3. Shake the jar 20–30 minutes. Your children will enjoy taking turns doing this step. (See next page for fun shaking ideas.) At first, the cream will coat the sides of the jar, but then you will see it pull away from the sides and take on a firmer consistency as it forms lumps of butter.
4. Empty the jar into a colander to separate the butter from the buttermilk. Dispose of the buttermilk, unless you plan to use it for another recipe.
5. Put the butter in a bowl and cover it with cold water. Empty the bowl into the colander to rinse the butter. This is to remove any extra buttermilk, which will make your butter taste sour.
6. Put the butter back into the bowl and gently stir in the salt, if you like.

7. Scoop the butter with a spoon into an ice cube tray and refrigerate for one hour. You should have about ½ cup butter or enough to fill at least 6 ice cube squares halfway.
8. Enjoy the homemade butter on toast, waffles, pancakes, or muffins.

Parent Tip

Here are some fun ways for your children to shake the jar:

- Have them sit in a circle and roll the jar to one another.
- Have them hop, skip, or jump while holding the jar.
- Put the jar in a backpack, put on some lively music, and have your kids dance while taking turns wearing the backpack.
- Set a timer for one minute and have one child shake the jar. When the minute is up, set the timer again and let another child shake the jar for one minute.

Homemade Applesauce

This recipe may be perfect for your baby, and your older children will definitely love it, too!

5 medium apples
½ cup water
Pinch of cinnamon

1. Wash the apples, then peel them. Your toddler and preschooler can help do these tasks, respectively.
2. Core the apples, then dice them. Your school-age child can do this second task.
3. Combine the diced apples, water, and cinnamon in a large saucepan and bring to a gentle boil. Lower heat and simmer for 4 minutes.
4. Use a potato masher to crush the diced apples. Simmer for 2 more minutes, until the mixture is the consistency of a sauce.
5. Place in a bowl and allow to cool in the refrigerator overnight. This recipe makes 4–6 servings.

S'mores Creatures

Your children will love making these tasty creatures!

2 graham crackers
2 chocolate squares
2 chocolate chips
1 large marshmallow

1. Set a graham cracker on a paper plate, then top with the chocolate squares.
2. Place a marshmallow on top of the chocolate squares. Set the chocolate chips on top of the marshmallow to make eyes.
3. Microwave the creature for 10–15 seconds or until the marshmallow starts to puff up.
4. Remove it from the microwave and watch the creature shrink. Top with another graham cracker and enjoy! This recipe makes one creature.

Sweet-and-Salty Snack

This treat is easy and fun to make.

1 dozen miniature pretzel twists
1 dozen Hershey's Kisses candies

1. Preheat your oven to 350°F.
2. Place the pretzels on a baking sheet in equally spaced rows. Your school-age child can do this step.
3. Your preschooler can unwrap the Kisses, and your toddler can place one on each pretzel.
4. Bake the treats for 1–2 minutes or until the Kisses begin to melt.

Splendid Smoothies

These refreshing and healthy smoothies are just as delightful to make as they are to drink!

½ cup fruit, such as bananas, blueberries, strawberries, and raspberries
½ scoop frozen vanilla yogurt
½ cup milk

1. Select the fruit to include in the smoothie. (If each child has a different preference, you may want to make a separate smoothie for each.) Wash the fruit in a colander. Your toddler can help with this task.
2. Slice the fruit into small pieces. Your preschooler can help with this step using a butter knife or even a spoon.
3. Place the frozen yogurt, milk, and fruit slices in a blender and blend on the fastest speed or the "liquefy" setting until there are no lumps. This is a good task for your school-age child.
4. Pour the smoothie into a glass or cup and enjoy! This recipe makes 1¼ cups.

Pineapple Pops

These healthy freezer pops will make your kids smile!

Pineapple rings (1 per child)
Vanilla or plain yogurt (about 3 large spoonfuls per child)
Wide Popsicle sticks (1 per child)

1. Line a large baking sheet with wax paper.
2. Lay the pineapple rings (up to four) on the wax paper. Your toddler can help with this task.
3. Insert a Popsicle stick into the side of each ring and push it through until the stick is halfway across the hole. This is a good task for your preschooler.
4. Spoon yogurt onto the pineapple rings to fill the holes and cover the rings. Your school-age child can do this step.
5. Freeze the pops overnight.

CHAPTER 11
Seasons & Holidays

During holidays, my kids love to eat sugary treats and swap gifts. But I found what they treasure most are the family traditions we celebrate.

—Lisa

Celebrating holidays and seasonal changes is a great way to strengthen family bonds. In this chapter, we include fun activities that commemorate both traditional and unusual occasions—from Thanksgiving to National Bubble Week. With these themed arts-and-crafts projects, games, and activities, we encourage you to treat each holiday and season as an opportunity to share family traditions or create new ones with your children.

Feel-Good New Year's Fortunes

Use this variation of an ancient Chinese tradition to look toward a bright future for your children on New Year's Day!

What You'll Need	All Ages	Baby	Toddler	Preschooler	School-Age Child
Fortunetelling items (see below)	🖐				
Index cards	🖐				
Pencil	🖐				
Scarf or blindfold				🖐	🖐

Before calling your children for the game, gather a number of various household items. For each item, write a symbolic "fortune" on an index card. Here are some examples of potential items and their possible fortunes:

- Pencil: *For a future writer or storyteller who has a vivid imagination and loves to share ideas.*
- Book: *For a future scholar, teacher, or historian who is curious and loves to help others.*
- Spoon: *For a future chef, baker, or musician who is creative, brave, and self-assured.*
- Paintbrush: *For a future artist who appreciates the beauty in everything.*

Keep your children's interests in mind as you select items. For instance, if your toddler is fascinated with firefighters, add a fire truck and write, "For a future firefighter who is brave, strong, and helpful."

When you finish the cards, fold them in half and place them under each corresponding item. Then call in your children. Don't tell them what each item represents, but have them take turns picking an item. Your baby and toddler can motion toward or point to their items, but you may choose to blindfold your preschooler and school-age child to heighten the mystery. When everyone has an object, you or your school-age child can read the cards to reveal the fortunes. If you like, replace the items on the table and play again. Or have your children find new items and come up with their own predictions for each one.

Parent Tip
Don't underestimate the power of suggestive messages. Need your children to remember to feed the dog? Put out the dog's food bowl with a fortune of "For a wonderful caregiver to all creatures…including your own dog!"

Groundhog Day Silhouettes

Groundhog Day is a traditional yet quirky way to predict the arrival of spring. Your kids can celebrate the holiday with this fun shadow activity.

What You'll Need	All Ages	Baby	Toddler	Preschooler	School-Age Child
Flashlight	🖐				
Black paper	🖐				
Tape	🖐				
Chalk	🖐				
Child-safe scissors	🖐				

Have each of your children take a turn standing in profile in front of a flashlight beam and casting a shadow onto a sheet of black paper taped to the wall. Make sure each sheet is level with the top of each child's head. Use chalk to trace around the shadow, then cut out the silhouette for a wonderful display!

Baby

Try sitting your baby in her highchair or ExerSaucer to trace her shadow. To keep her facing in profile, encourage her siblings to stand in front of her and make funny faces, sing, and call out her name. Don't worry if she moves around, though—close enough is good enough! Another way to get a great

silhouette of your baby (and your other children, too) is to lay
her on the paper and trace around her body.

Toddler

Your toddler may also have trouble sitting still while you trace
his shadow. To help keep him still and amused, ask an older
child to read the toddler's favorite book out loud while standing in front of him. When his silhouette is finished, ask him to
point out his nose, mouth, chin, and other features.

Preschooler

At this age, your preschooler will not only sit still for his turn,
but he'll also help with the activity. He can cut out his silhouette with child-safe scissors. He may also want to hold the
flashlight steady as his siblings' silhouettes are drawn. After
everyone's silhouette is finished, see if your preschooler can
identify each one. Ask him how he came to his conclusions.

School-Age Child

Your school-age child can help a lot with this activity. She can
tape the paper to the wall, hold the flashlight, and help cut out
the silhouettes. She can even trace her siblings' shadows. If
you like, ask her to write her wishes for the upcoming spring
on the back of her silhouette. Talk about what she can do to
make them come true!

You're in My Heart

Show some love with your kids by creating a colorful clay heart together!

What You'll Need	All Ages	Baby	Toddler	Preschooler	School-Age Child
Homemade clay (see recipe on page 364)	🖐				
Baking sheet	🖐				
Cooking spray	🖐				
Zip-close plastic bag		🖐			
Marker	🖐				
Butter knife	🖐				
Pencil	🖐				
Yarn	🖐				

Your children can help make the clay. Then have your kids work together to flatten the red clay on a greased baking sheet so the clay is one to two inches thick. Draw a large heart on the clay with a marker, then cut out the heart shape with a butter knife. Next, your kids can decorate the heart by forming small letters, shapes, or designs with the purple clay and pressing them gently onto the surface of the heart. Tell them this represents how each of them are in the gift receiver's heart!

When they're done, make a hole at the top of the heart with a pencil so you can loop a string through it later for displaying. Bake the heart for 30 to 40 minutes at 300°F until the exterior of the dough has formed a crust. When finished, you'll have a decorative heart to display!

Baby
While the other children work on the activity, give your baby a zip-close plastic bag of clay to hold and squeeze. If she is younger than six months, guide her hands to help her explore a piece of clay. Press her fingers into it, but make sure she doesn't place it in her mouth. You may even want to press her fingers into the heart so she can add her own "decoration."

Toddler
Your toddler will love to pound, tear, and push the clay, which will strengthen his hand muscles. Help him decide what purple designs to add to the heart, then show him how to press them in gently.

Preschooler
When making the clay, include your preschooler as much as possible. Measuring the ingredients, pouring the liquids, and stirring the dough are great ways for him to learn early math skills and how to follow directions.

School-Age Child
Let your school-age child play a large role in preparing the clay, and perhaps let her cut the heart shape with the butter knife. Once the heart is done, she may also want to make her

own hearts or other shapes using the leftover clay. Perhaps she will want to enlist her siblings' help.

Homemade Clay
1½ cup of salt
4 cups of flour
1½ cups of water
Red and blue food coloring

Mix the salt and flour in a bowl with a spoon. Add water gradually. When dough forms, knead it well, adding water if it's too crumbly or flour if it's too sticky. It should be firm. Divide the clay into two bowls. Mix red food coloring in one bowl. Mix blue and red food coloring (to make purple) in the other bowl.

At the End of a Rainbow

For Saint Patrick's Day, make a rainbow windsock complete with a trail of dazzling gold coins!

What You'll Need	All Ages	Baby	Toddler	Preschooler	School-Age Child
Child-safe scissors	🖐				
Thin cardboard	🖐				
Yellow paint, yellow crayons, and yellow tissue paper and glue	🖐				
Construction paper in rainbow colors			🖐	🖐	🖐
Stapler			🖐	🖐	🖐
Hole punch			🖐	🖐	🖐
Yarn			🖐	🖐	🖐
Paintbrush		🖐	🖐		
Green paint		🖐			
Wet wipes		🖐			

Cut several circles, each about two inches in diameter, from thin cardboard. Give each child some cardboard circles to decorate with yellow paint, yellow crayons, or yellow tissue paper and glue. Set these gold coins aside when finished.

To make the windsock, roll a sheet of green construction paper lengthwise to create a tube. Staple the edges together to hold the tube's shape. You and your older children can then cut 1-inch-wide strips from construction paper in rainbow colors. Staple one end of each strip to the tube so they dangle from the bottom. Next, punch a hole at the bottom of each strip and at the top of each coin. Using yarn, tie each coin to a strip. Lastly, punch a hole at the top of the tube and string it with yarn so you can display the windsock outside or inside your home.

Baby

Give your baby a cardboard coin to hold and examine. If you like, help her create a shamrock design on it: Fold her hand into a fist, then paint the pinky-side edge of her hand green. Press her hand onto the coin three times to create a three-leaf clover shape. Use wet wipes to clean her hand when you're done.

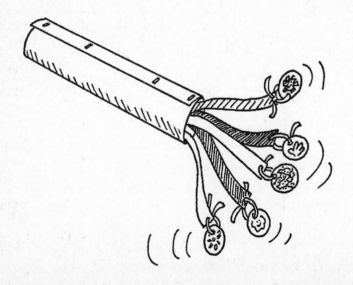

Toddler

When your toddler is decorating her coins, help her use a paintbrush to spread glue onto them. She can then press pieces of yellow tissue paper onto the glue.

Preschooler

Your preschooler can give his coin a textured look. Have him dunk a 2-inch length of yarn in the yellow paint. He can coil the yarn on top of the coin in a squiggly spiral, then press the yarn to release the paint. Encourage him to repeat this process until he has covered his coin in paint.

School-Age Child

As the family works on the windsock, challenge your school-age child with a few mathematical questions using the coins. For example, ask, "If you have ten coins, your sister took three away, and then your brother gave you two, how many would you have?" She can use the coins to visually figure out the answers.

 Did You Know?
Gold coins are one of the oldest forms of money, dating back to 560 BC.

Leprechaun Race

Search for homemade gold coins in a game that will get your kids moving.

What You'll Need	All Ages	Baby	Toddler	Preschooler	School-Age Child
Large paper bag or box	🖐				
Yellow construction paper	🖐				
Child-safe scissors	🖐				
Marker	🖐				

To prepare for this activity, find a large paper bag or box to serve as the "pot." Then you and your children can make two or three gold "coins" for each child by cutting circles about three inches in diameter from yellow construction paper. On the back of each coin, write simple instructions your children can do. For example:

- *Point to your belly.*
- *Clap your hands.*
- *Tap your ears.*
- *Turn around.*
- *Reach for the sky.*
- *Wave your hands.*

- *Shake your neighbor's hand.*
- *Smile and stand still like a statue.*
- *Pretend to dig for gold.*

While the children wait, hide the coins in a room, making sure to stash some in places your younger kids can find. When you're done, tell your children to find as many coins as they can and put them into the pot. When your kids have found all the coins, have each one take a turn picking a coin from the pot. As you or your school-age child reads the back of the coin, encourage everyone to follow the instructions!

Baby

Accompany your baby during the coin hunt. If she is mobile, direct her toward a coin within her reach. She can retrieve it and drop it into the pot. Also help her follow the instructions on the coins, if needed. But she may surprise you by watching the others and following some instructions herself, like finding her belly or reaching up high!

Toddler

Your toddler will gain confidence as she finds coins. If she needs a little direction, point her toward the general location, such as, "Look near the toy box." Finding the coins, putting them into the pot, and following the instructions will strengthen your toddler's abilities to listen and concentrate. Give her lots of encouragement as she completes these tasks.

Preschooler

Your preschooler will search enthusiastically for coins around the room. To challenge him in a different way, however, give him special instructions: Before he can drop a coin in the pot, he must turn it over and identify three letters from the sentence. Once he calls the letters out loud, he can drop the coin and return to the search.

School-Age Child

Your school-age child may enjoy reading the instructions on each coin out loud to the group. If you like, you can read the instructions, and tell him he has a special rule: He can follow the instructions only if he first hears the phrase, "The leprechaun says…" This activity will encourage careful listening, especially because his siblings will be following the instructions regardless of the preface!

Doing the Bubble Pop

Celebrated around the first day of spring, National Bubble Week is the perfect time to play with bubbles.

What You'll Need	All Ages	Baby	Toddler	Preschooler	School-Age Child
Nontoxic bubble solution	👋				
Plastic wands	👋				
Drinking straws				👋	👋
Household objects, such as paper clips, spatulas, paper plates, and so on					👋
Kiddie pool and Hula-Hoop					👋

All kids love to blow bubbles, and yours are sure to be no exception!

Baby

Your baby will love to track the bubbles as they drift by and eventually pop. When he is around six months old, he may try to grab them. To help him "catch" a bubble, wet his hand with the bubble solution, taking care that he doesn't put it in his mouth. Blow a bubble his way and help him hold his hand out to catch it. He may be able to touch the bubble for a moment before it pops!

Toddler

Your toddler may be ready to blow his first bubbles. Have him dip the wand into the bubble solution, then slowly pull it out. Show him how to make an O shape with his lips, then gently blow on the bubble solution. Offer to hold his wand on his first couple of tries.

Preschooler

Teach your preschooler how to blow a double bubble: Blow a bubble and gently catch it on the wand. Have your preschooler dip a straw into the bubble solution and slowly insert it into the bubble. Because the straw is wet, it shouldn't pop the bubble. Once inside, have her gently blow into the straw. Did she create a double bubble? This experiment may take several tries and will exercise her motor skills, concentration, and patience!

School-Age Child

Your school-age child can make her own wands from household objects. For instance, she can twist and mold a paper clip to resemble a wand. Other possibilities include straws, spatulas with holes, and plastic plates with holes cut in them. To make the ultimate bubble, take this activity outside. Cover the bottom of a kiddie pool with bubble solution and have her use a Hula-Hoop as a wand!

Signs of Spring

Plastic eggs and natural objects make for a fun guessing game!

What You'll Need	All Ages	Baby	Toddler	Preschooler	School-Age Child
Small baskets (or bags)	🖐				
Brightly colored plastic eggs	🖐				
Cereal		🖐			

Give your children each a basket and several plastic eggs. Tell them to search outside for small natural objects to put in the eggs, such as rocks, leaves, grass, pine needles, acorns, bark, puddle water, mud, and more. When they're done, have them gather for a guessing game. Each child will shake an egg, and the siblings will to try to guess its contents. If the object doesn't make a noise when shaken, the child can give the siblings a hint. For example, he can say, "Inside is something squirrels like to eat!" After the siblings have guessed, the child can open the egg carefully to reveal the object.

Baby

The shape and bright colors of plastic eggs will appeal to babies. If your baby is eating solids, fill an egg with cereal. While her siblings hunt for objects to put in their eggs, she will enjoy shaking her egg, then eating the snack inside. If your baby isn't yet eating solids, give her a tour of the outdoors as you search for objects to put in eggs for her. Point out blossoming flowers, chirping birds, and the blue sky.

Toddler
Rather than hunt for objects, your toddler may prefer to load and unload her eggs into and out of the basket. Show her how to pull an egg apart and snap it back together. Encourage her to scoop up small pebbles into an egg. She'll enjoy shaking it during the guessing game.

Preschooler
Your preschooler will enjoy searching for objects for the guessing game. To challenge him, describe a fairly visible nature object, such as a white rock, and ask him to find it and put it in an egg.

School-Age Child
Your school-age child will be busy collecting objects. For a special assignment, give him the task of collecting objects whose names begin with a letter in the word *spring*. For example:

Sand
Pine cone
Rock
Insect
Nut (acorn)
Grass

The Great Easter Egg Search

Add your own twist to an outdoor Easter egg hunt!

What You'll Need	All Ages	Baby	Toddler	Preschooler	School-Age Child
Plastic eggs (one color per child)	🖐				
Treats for eggs, including love notes, animal crackers, Goldfish crackers, stickers, and so on			🖐	🖐	🖐
Baskets	🖐				
Ribbon		🖐			
Chalk				🖐	🖐

Fill plastic eggs with age-appropriate treats for your toddler, preschooler, and school-age child. Then hide the eggs around your yard. Designate a different color for each child so your children will know which eggs have been filled just for them!

Baby

Babies love to handle colorful plastic eggs. If your baby is older than six months, set him next to a small basket filled with empty eggs. He may take out one egg at a time, or he may decide to dump the basket and fill it up again. If your baby is younger than six months, entertain him with an egg bobber during the egg hunt: Tape ribbon to an empty egg and dangle the egg near your baby's hands, letting him try to grab it.

Toddler

Place your toddler's eggs in fairly visible locations, give him a basket, and send him off on the hunt! After he's collected the eggs, help him count them. Encourage him to open and shut them to help build his motor skills—and to find the treats inside.

Preschooler and School-Age Child

Hide your preschooler's and school-age child's eggs in both easy and challenging locations. Give them baskets, then draw chalk maps to their eggs on the sidewalk or driveway. Provide orientation. For example, say, "This is our house. This is the front porch and the driveway. The eggs I want you to find are right here." Draw an *X* on the location. This activity will help your children's ability to follow directions and identify locations. For fun, let your children hide an egg and draw a map for you to find it.

> My toddler created his own game with the eggs. He enjoyed opening the eggs and finding the treasures, but he had a hard time closing an egg once it was opened. He decided to put a few treasures on a Frisbee and place the egg halves on top of them. He loved lifting the eggs to find his treasures all over again!
>
> —Lisa

Cinco de Mayo Piñatas

Celebrate this festive Mexican holiday with homemade piñatas.

What You'll Need	All Ages	Baby	Toddler	Preschooler	School-Age Child
Paper lunch bags			✋	✋	✋
Crayons			✋	✋	✋
Fun items, such as soft or plastic toys, age-appropriate candy, and so on			✋	✋	✋
Tape			✋	✋	✋
String			✋	✋	✋
Scarf or handkerchief to use as a blindfold			✋	✋	✋
Plastic bat			✋	✋	✋
Large paper bag		✋			
Baby toy		✋			

Give your toddler, preschooler, and school-age child each a paper lunch bag to decorate with crayons. When the bags are decorated, help your kids fill them with fun, unbreakable items from around the house, then tape them closed. Hang each piñata by taping string to it and tying the string to a clothesline or a low tree branch. One by one, blindfold the children, spin them slowly, then encourage them to try to break open their piñatas with a plastic bat.

Baby

While your older kids make the piñatas, use a large paper bag to entertain your baby. If he is six months or older, lay the bag on its side and place a favorite toy inside it. Set him next to the open end of the bag and encourage him to retrieve the toy. If your baby is younger than six months, place him on his tummy and have him use his neck muscles to get a peak inside the bag. For a fun peekaboo game, hide an object under the bag, then lift up the bag quickly to reveal the toy.

Toddler

At this age, your toddler will enjoy seeing what items fit into the bag just as much as she'll enjoy decorating it. She will probably fill and empty her bag several times. When it's time to break open the piñatas, she may need your assistance with the plastic bat.

Preschooler and School-Age Child

Encourage your preschooler and school-age child to decorate their piñatas as people, animals, or their favorite characters. They may spend a long time decorating their piñatas and a short time breaking them open!

Did You Know?
Cinco de Mayo commemorates the victory of Mexican forces on May 5, 1862. Today, Mexicans celebrate the day with parades and speeches.

A Child's Touch Bracelet

This Mother's Day charm bracelet will forever capture each child's unique fingerprint.

What You'll Need	All Ages	Baby	Toddler	Preschooler	School-Age Child
Quick-drying molding clay in different colors	🖐				
Toothpicks	🖐				
String	🖐				

Let your children each choose a color of clay, then flatten a nickel-size piece of each color until it's a half inch thick. Gently press each child's fingerprint into a clay piece, rolling the finger side to side firmly to capture the print. Use a toothpick to poke a hole in the top of each clay piece, then use the toothpick to inscribe each child's initials on the back of their respective charms. After the clay hardens overnight, help your older children thread the pieces onto string to make a bracelet.

Baby

At the beginning of the activity, show the different colors of clay to your baby. Be sure to name each color. Perhaps she will coo or squeal to signal her preference! Let her siblings decide which color she likes best. Before pressing her fingertip into the clay, let her feel it. She will love to explore the texture with her hands, but make sure she doesn't put the clay into her mouth.

Toddler, Preschooler, and School-Age Child

After taking your children's fingerprints, ask them to help you choose a safe place for the charms to dry overnight. Then let them play with the remaining clay. Your toddler may just enjoy squeezing and pounding the material, but your preschooler and school-age child may create figures and shapes for Mother's Day presents. Once the clay has hardened overnight, your pre-schooler and school-age child can help thread the charms onto the string, then help wrap the gift for Mom.

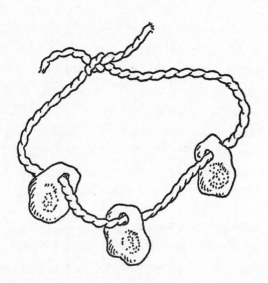

Mother's Day Window Box

Your children can create a special window box of flowers that will last forever. No need to water!

What You'll Need	All Ages	Baby	Toddler	Preschooler	School-Age Child
Scissors	🖐				
Cardboard egg carton	🖐				
Play dough	🖐				
Pencil		🖐	🖐	🖐	
Construction paper		🖐	🖐	🖐	
Pad of washable ink		🖐			
Glue sticks		🖐	🖐	🖐	
Popsicle sticks		🖐	🖐	🖐	
Child-safe scissors				🖐	
Tissue paper					🖐
Pipe cleaner					🖐

Cut the lid off an egg carton, then cut the bottom of the carton in half lengthwise so you have two long rows of egg cups. You'll need only one of these rows, so discard the other half—unless you have more than six children! Put some play dough in each egg cup. Your children can then make flowers to "plant" in the play dough. Make sure to write the child's name on each flower.

Baby

Your baby can also contribute to the window box. To create his flower, trace around his hand on construction paper and cut it out. To decorate the petals, press his fingertips onto an ink pad, then onto each finger of the cutout. Glue the bloom onto a Popsicle stick. Before you plant the flower in the carton, hold it up to the baby and count each "petal" out loud. Then take your baby's hand and count each of his fingers to help him make the connection between the flower and his hand.

Toddler

Help your toddler create a flower. Cut a circle from construction paper, then cut two triangles into the top to create a tulip. He can then glue a Popsicle stick to the bloom with your help. Your toddler will also enjoy helping you put play dough into the egg cups. Show him how to roll the dough into small balls. Dab glue onto the bottom of each egg cup, then have your toddler place a ball into each.

Preschooler

For your preschooler's own unique flower, have her draw different size circles on a piece of construction paper and cut them out. Using the largest circle as a base, she can glue the other circles slightly overlapping one another to create layered petals. When the bloom is finished, have her glue it onto a Popsicle stick.

School-Age Child

Help your school-age child follow these steps to make a three-dimensional bloom out of tissue paper:

1. Cut twelve squares, each five inches long and wide, from different colored tissue paper.
2. Stack the squares in the following pattern: square, diamond, square, diamond, and so on.
3. Place one hand under all the layers of the stack, then lift your index finger to create a peak in the middle.
4. Grasp the peak with the fingers and thumb of your other hand (making sure to grasp all the layers at once), and twist the peak to form a knob.
5. Wrap one end of a pipe cleaner around the knob to create a stem.
6. Lastly, unfurl the tissue paper layers to create petals. Voilà! A beautiful, full flower!

Parent Tip

Spray the flowers with a pleasing scent. We recommend lavender to bring a sense of peace and harmony. You can also use perfume.

Patriotic Wreath

Celebrate Memorial Day with this homemade star wreath.

What You'll Need	All Ages	Baby	Toddler	Preschooler	School-Age Child
Child-safe scissors			🖐	🖐	🖐
White construction paper			🖐	🖐	🖐
Cotton balls	🖐				
Red tissue paper	🖐				
Blue painter's tape	🖐				
Glue sticks			🖐	🖐	🖐
Paper plate			🖐	🖐	🖐

Prepare for this activity with your children by cutting out nine stars, four inches across, from white construction paper. Give your toddler, preschooler, and school-age child three stars each and instruct each of them to decorate one star with white cotton balls, one with red tissue paper, and one with blue painter's tape. When they are done, help them glue the finished stars around the edge of a paper plate to create a patriotic wreath.

Baby

Let your baby explore the art supplies on her highchair tray while her siblings decorate their stars. She will enjoy the soft cotton balls, the crinkly tissue paper, and the sticky painter's tape. When the wreath is finished, have your children show it to your baby—she will enjoy gazing at the colors and patterns.

Toddler
Assist your toddler with his stars. For his white and red stars, dab glue on the cotton balls and pieces of tissue paper, then let him press them onto the stars. For his blue star, tear off small pieces of tape and let him pull the pieces from your fingers and press them onto the star.

Preschooler
After everyone has decorated their stars, your preschooler will enjoy picking a pattern for gluing them onto the paper plate. For example, she may suggest that the blue stars go together, followed by the red ones, and then the white ones. Or she may suggest alternating individual red, white, and blue stars around the plate.

School-Age Child
Show your school-age child how to make a textured star. He can roll the tissue paper into small balls, dot them with glue, and place them close together on the star. He can also pull apart the cotton balls slightly, then press them onto a glue-covered star to create a wispy look. Lastly, he can create squares across his star with the tape.

Wave That Flag

Proudly creating a homemade American flag as a family is a great way to celebrate Flag Day.

What You'll Need	All Ages	Baby	Toddler	Preschooler	School-Age Child
Large blue and white sheets of construction paper	🖐				
Child-safe scissors	🖐				
Glue stick	🖐				
Red and yellow tissue paper	🖐				
Paintbrush	🖐				
Watered-down glue (2 parts water to 1 part glue)	🖐				
Marker	🖐				

To make the flag, help your older children follow these instructions. Your baby will enjoy watching her siblings busily work with such bright art supplies!

1. From a sheet of blue construction paper, cut a rectangle roughly a quarter of the size of the sheet. Glue the rectangle onto the upper left corner of a white sheet of construction paper.
2. Rip yellow tissue paper into twenty small pieces and tear red tissue paper into seven long strips.

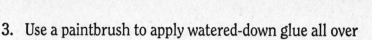

3. Use a paintbrush to apply watered-down glue all over the flag.
4. Press the yellow tissue paper pieces onto the blue rectangle to make stars.
5. Starting at the bottom of the sheet, lay the red tissue paper strips horizontally at equal distances on the white part of the flag. Trim the top strips to accommodate the blue rectangle.
6. To preserve the flag (and add shine), brush watered-down glue on the tissue paper.
7. After the glue has dried, use a marker to record words that your children use to describe their country and the people who protect it.

As you make the flag together, consider doing the following activities:

- Sing patriotic songs like "The Star-Spangled Banner" and "You're a Grand Old Flag." Your younger children will love hearing everyone's voices and may try to "sing" along!
- Explain the significance of the stars and stripes on the American flag. Point out that while your homemade flag has twenty stars, the real flag has fifty—one for each state.
- Provide a world map or globe and point out the United States. Then point out your state and town. Encourage them to explore the other countries on the map.

Day in the Life of Daddy

On Father's Day, your children can pay tribute to their dad or father figure with this special performance!

What You'll Need	All Ages	Baby	Toddler	Preschooler	School-Age Child
A few of Dad's shirts, ties, hats, and shoes	✋				

Tell your children they're going to perform a show about their dad or a special father figure. Ask them each what they love to do with him, and have them recall the tasks he does every day (for example, shaving his face or mowing the lawn). Have them each choose (or help them choose) one of those tasks or actions to perform. Then let them get into costume by choosing some of Dad's clothes to wear over their clothes, while you fetch the guest of honor. When the audience and performers are ready, let the show begin!

Baby

Your baby can look the part by wearing one of his dad's hats. If he's old enough to play an interactive game with Dad, like rolling a ball back and forth, have one of your other children play the baby's part, and let "Dad" and "the baby" roll the ball to each other.

Toddler

Your toddler will love dressing up in his dad's shirt and tie. When it's his turn to perform, have him do something he associates with his dad. For example, turn on Dad's favorite music and let your toddler dance, if he and his dad like to cut a rug together. Or have him "read" a favorite book to his teddy bear, if he and his dad enjoy story time.

Preschooler

Your preschooler may enjoy walking in her dad's shoes. Let her reenact parts of Dad's day according to his different shoes. For example, while wearing her dad's dressy work shoes, she can pretend to type on a computer and answer the phone. Then she can put on Dad's sneakers and pretend to mow the lawn.

School-Age Child

Your school-age child can reenact an entire sequence of events in her dad's daily life. For example, she can put on a pair of Dad's pajamas, then pretend to shave, change into work clothes, comb her hair, read the paper, drink a cup of coffee, let out the dog, kiss the kids goodbye, and more.

Parent Tip

You may want to preserve this performance, so have a camera or camcorder handy. Your children's reenactments of their dad's life may keep him in stitches for years to come!

Summer Solstice Sun Catchers

Make colorful sun catchers to greet the summer sunshine on the longest day of the year!

What You'll Need	All Ages	Baby	Toddler	Preschooler	School-Age Child
Clear contact paper		🖐	🖐		
Colored tissue paper		🖐	🖐		🖐
Child-safe scissors		🖐	🖐		🖐
Clear plastic lids from deli containers, to-go tubs, and so on				🖐	🖐
Permanent markers in at least three colors				🖐	🖐
Yarn or ribbon					🖐
Hole punch					🖐

While you create sun catchers for your baby and toddler, your older kids can make their own. Hang the finished sun catchers with yarn near a light source and watch the colors dance!

Baby

If your baby is six months or older, give him a sheet of clear contact paper to touch. He'll enjoy the sticky sensation. Afterward, lay ripped-up pieces of light-colored tissue paper on the contact paper, then cover it with another sheet of contact paper. Cut out a circle or other shape for your baby's very own sun catcher. As the sun shines through the sun catcher, the dazzling colors will delight your baby, no matter what his age!

Toddler

Set a sheet of contact paper sticky side up in front of your toddler and have her press a piece of tissue paper onto it. Have her stick on a second piece of tissue paper so it overlaps the first piece, then show her how to hold the contact paper up to the light to see the colors glow. Encourage her to overlap different colors of paper in pairs to create new colors—red over blue makes purple and yellow over red makes orange. When she's finished, place another sheet of contact paper on the tissue paper, then ask her what shape she'd like you to cut out for the final sun catcher. Your toddler can then help you find the perfect spot to hang it.

Preschooler

Give your preschooler a large, clear plastic lid and encourage him to color one side of it completely. Show him how to make colored spirals by drawing one continuous circle that begins around the perimeter of the lid then becomes smaller and smaller as he reaches the center. If he likes, he can switch the color of marker along the way.

School-Age Child

Your school-age child can follow the same directions as your preschooler. She can further decorate her sun catcher by adding colorful tails to the bottom. Have her cut ribbons, yarn, or thin strips of tissue paper in various lengths. To secure them to her catcher, she can use a hole punch to create holes at the base of the lid. She can then tie the decorations to it.

Seashell Magnets

Nothing says summer like seashells, so use them to create magnets you can enjoy season after season.

What You'll Need	All Ages	Baby	Toddler	Preschooler	School-Age Child
Seashells (from beach or local craft store)	🖐				
Sponges or old toothbrushes			🖐	🖐	🖐
Washable tempera paint and paintbrushes			🖐	🖐	🖐
Mineral or baby oil			🖐	🖐	🖐
Magnetic tape			🖐	🖐	🖐
Quick-drying glue		🖐			
Empty egg carton		🖐			
School glue				🖐	🖐
Construction paper				🖐	🖐
Child-safe scissors				🖐	🖐

To begin, show your older children how to gently clean the seashells with water and a sponge or old toothbrush. When the shells are dry, your children can decorate them with paint. If your kids prefer a natural look, they can use their fingers to wipe the shells with mineral or baby oil to make them shine. When they are done, affix magnetic tape to the back of each shell.

Baby

Seashells have many different textures, which make them attractive to your curious baby's hands. For safe exploration, glue clean seashells without jagged edges into the cups of an empty egg carton. For an auditory experience, hold a large seashell to your baby's ear. Does she react to the sound?

Toddler

Your toddler will enjoy exploring large seashells (smaller ones pose a choking hazard) before he paints them. Can he hear noise when he holds a shell to his ear? Have him describe what each shell feels like. Is it bumpy or smooth? What color is it?

Preschooler and School-Age Child

Your preschooler and school-age child can create seashell animals. To make a dog, for example, they can paint on eyes and a mouth. They can then glue a small pair of brown construction paper triangles to the top of the shell for ears and a small brown strip on the bottom for a tail.

Parent Tip

To learn more about shells, read with your kids the delightful picture book *Shells! Shells! Shells!* by Nancy Elizabeth Wallace.

Grandparents Day Video

Create a special video displaying each child's accomplishments for their grandparents or "grandfriends."

What You'll Need	All Ages	Baby	Toddler	Preschooler	School-Age Child
Camcorder	✋				
Your children displaying their talents!	✋				

Grab the camcorder and tell your children you will record a special video for their grandparents. Let your children decide what they would like to do on the video. Some age-appropriate suggestions are below.

Baby

Be sure to get a close-up of your baby, noting any characteristics that bear resemblance to his grandparents. Try to capture a smile by singing his favorite song or having a sibling play peekaboo with him. Your other children can serve as "directors" encouraging your baby to show off recent accomplishments such as sitting up or rolling over.

Toddler

Your toddler is beginning to gain more control of her art utensils. Record her coloring or creating other artwork you can send along with the video. Ask her to describe the artwork on camera for her grandparents.

Preschooler

Your preschooler is learning about the letters in his name, and he may even be able to write them for his proud grandparents. You can also record any thoughts or special memories of times he has enjoyed with his grandparents.

School-Age Child

Interview your school-age child about her favorite sports, classes at school, and friendships. Try to ask open-ended questions. She may also want to write and recite a poem about how special her grandparents are to her.

Did You Know?
In 1978, President Jimmy Carter proclaimed National Grandparents Day would be celebrated every year on the first Sunday after Labor Day.

Apple Taste Test

Autumn is the perfect time to taste all kinds of apples!

What You'll Need	All Ages	Baby	Toddler	Preschooler	School-Age Child
Several kinds of apples, such as Granny Smith, McIntosh, and Golden Delicious	🖐				
Paring knife and fork	🖐				
Paper					🖐
Pencil					🖐

If possible, take your kids to a local apple orchard and pick a variety of apples together. If visiting an orchard isn't possible, buy various kinds of apples at the supermarket. At home, gather your children for a taste test. Before eating the apples, your older kids can examine them and describe their differences. Then serve a piece of each apple to each child (in age-appropriate servings). Discuss its taste and have your school-age child record his siblings' votes on a special chart.

Baby

If your baby is eating fruit, her vote counts, too! Have her try a tiny bit of each apple after it's been peeled, sliced, and mashed with a fork. (McIntosh is a good choice to start with because of its appealing, sweet taste.) Does she seem to enjoy it? Have your other children decide. If your baby isn't eating fruits yet, have a sibling hold an apple slice in front of her to see if she reacts to its color and smell. You can record a coo or a smile on the chart!

397

Toddler

Give your toddler a few bite-size pieces of the different apples. Even the pickiest toddler will likely try apples, although your toddler may show you he doesn't care for a specific variety by spitting it out! This activity is also a great opportunity to teach colors. Help him identify the color of each apple.

Preschooler

Have your preschooler try each apple variety sliced or whole, with or without peel. Adjectives are becoming a huge part of his vocabulary. Use this activity to encourage him to describe the look and taste of each apple. For example, he may use words like *sweet*, *crunchy*, *soft*, or *chewy* to express his thoughts.

School-Age Child

To make the taste-test chart, your school-age child can create one as shown below. He can list the name of each apple variety down a sheet of paper, then record each sibling's name across the top. As each sibling tastes each apple, your school-age child can record the response with a smiley face or a frowning face. Don't let him forget to taste the apples himself and record his reactions!

Sample Taste-Test Chart				
	Jake	Brooke	Kyle	Noah
McIntosh	☺	☹	☺	☹
Granny Smith	☹	☺	☹	☺
Golden Delicious	☺	☹	☺	☺

Leaf Place Mats

Autumn leaves will make beautiful place settings for the whole family.

What You'll Need	All Ages	Baby	Toddler	Preschooler	School-Age Child
Fallen leaves	🖐				
Scissors	🖐				
Paper grocery bags	🖐				
Glue sticks		🖐	🖐		
Washable tempera paint				🖐	🖐
Paintbrushes				🖐	🖐
Clear contact paper	🖐				
Ribbon and hole punch		🖐			
Crayons					🖐

On a pleasant autumn day, you and your children can gather a variety of fallen leaves. When inside, cut paper grocery bags into 8-inch-by-11-inch rectangles for your toddler, preschooler, and school-age child. Your children can then glue leaves onto these homemade place mats or lightly paint leaves and press the imprints onto the mats. When the finished place mats are dry, cover them with clear contact paper and trim the excess.

Baby

As your older children make the place mats, make your baby a bib from the same materials. Cut a bib shape from a paper bag. Show her some brightly colored leaves and describe their colors:

"This leaf is yellow; this leaf is orange." See if she coos or reaches for her favorites. Glue the leaves to her bib, cover it with contact paper, and use ribbon and a hole punch to secure it around her neck. She should wear the bib only under your close supervision.

Toddler

Your toddler may enjoy gluing leaves onto the grocery bag with your help, but he may have an easier time creating his place mat if you skip the bag altogether. Instead, tape an 8-inch-by-11-inch sheet of clear contact paper sticky side up to the table and encourage him to stick the leaves directly to it. During this process, however, your toddler may discover that the dried leaves will often crumble if he tries to pull them off the contact paper or if he presses them on too roughly. If this happens, talk about cause and effect—and make sure he has lots of leaves! When he's done, cover his work with another sheet of contact paper.

Preschooler

At this age, your preschooler has the dexterity to paint one side of a leaf and press it onto her place mat. Encourage her to use different colors of paint and different shapes of leaves to create a design.

School-Age Child

For an added art challenge, encourage your school-age child to incorporate the leaf imprints into a drawing on his place mat. For instance, he can turn an imprint of a maple leaf into butterfly wings or an imprint of an oak leaf into the flames from a rocket.

Columbus Day Sailing Hats

To commemorate Christopher Columbus's voyage to America, set sail for fun with these easy-to-make sailor hats!

What You'll Need	All Ages	Baby	Toddler	Preschooler	School-Age Child
Newspaper	🖐				
Tape	🖐				
Decorations, including crayons, stickers, glue, feathers, and strips of colored paper	🖐				
Toy boat			🖐		
Paper towel tube				🖐	

From an old newspaper, pull out a spread (four pages, front and back) for each of your children. Your older children can help you fold the paper into sailing hats for themselves and their younger siblings. Here's how:

1. Close the spread at the vertical crease and turn the paper sideways so the open edge is on the bottom and the crease is at the top.
2. Fold down the top corners so they meet, then tape them together.

3. Fold the bottom edges up several inches all around the paper. (It may take several tries.)
4. Decorate the hat with crayons, stickers, feathers, and colored paper strips.

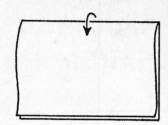

Baby

When your baby's hat is done, place it on his head, then seat him face-out on your lap and sing the song "Row, Row, Row Your Boat" with him. If you like, sing this fun version of the tune:

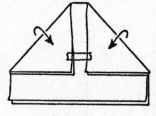

Sail, sail, sail your boat
in the ocean blue.
Merrily, merrily, Columbus sailed
in 1492.

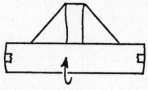

Toddler

While wearing his hat, your toddler can pretend to be a real sailor. Fill the kitchen sink or the bathtub and let him float a toy boat in it. Ask him about his sailing adventures: "Where is your boat going? Is your boat going slow or fast?"

Preschooler

To be a true explorer of the time, your preschooler should have his own telescope. Let him decorate a paper towel tube with stickers. Encourage him to use his imagination to locate objects at sea with his telescope.

School-Age Child

Your school-age child also can make three smaller hats from smaller sheets of paper to represent Columbus's three ships (the Niña, the Pinta, and the Santa Maria). Perhaps she'll choose to race them in the sink! Line up the ships on one side of the sink and give them each a gentle shove. Which one makes it to the other side first?

Parent Tip

If you find the hat is too big and falling over your child's face, simply place it on her head and pinch the back to create the ideal size. Then tape the bottom of the hat where you pinched it.

Spider Games

Build a big, soft spider for some active Halloween games!

What You'll Need	All Ages	Baby	Toddler	Preschooler	School-Age Child
Several large pillows	🖐				
8 large towels	🖐				

To create the spider's body, help your children pile pillows in the center of a room with lots of open space. Then roll up the towels and place them around the pillow pile to create the spider's eight legs. Have each child sit on a spider leg (place your baby in your lap as you sit on a leg) to play these games.

The Laughing Spider
Recite the following story together while tickling the spider legs:

This great big spider
has ticklish legs.
So we tickled,
and he laughed.
And then this great big spider
told us to jump into the bath!
(Everyone jumps onto the spider's body!)

Creepy, Creepy Spider
Have everyone sit in a circle. Choose one child to walk around the circle and tap each sibling she passes on the shoulder. As she does so, everyone recites:

Creepy, creepy spider,
climbing in the web,
tapped me on the shoulder—
I guess it's time for bed!

At the word *bed*, the last person tapped is out of the game and must move to the spider's body. Play again until there are no more shoulders to tap. Then choose a new person to tap shoulders.

Baby

When it's time to jump onto the spider's body during each game, gently move onto the pillows with your baby. The motion will excite him! The spider also creates a great tummy time experience for him: Lay your baby's chest over a rolled-up towel while supporting his hips. (If he does tummy time during "Creepy, Creepy Spider," you may want to move his towel far enough away so he's safe from the action but still close enough to watch his siblings play.)

Toddler

Before playing the games, let your toddler explore the spider legs. Encourage him to first step over the legs while you count them. On his next trip around, have him hold your hands while jumping over the legs and counting them with you. Come up with other ways to travel over the legs. These exercises will strengthen his coordination and muscles.

Preschooler

Let your preschooler take a leadership role during these games by encouraging her to keep the spider ready for action. She can make sure the legs are in place and the pillows are fluffed. She can also make sure everyone has a turn to tap shoulders during "Creepy, Creepy Spider."

School-Age Child

Instead of tickling the spider legs during "The Laughing Spider" game, your school-age child can show off her agility skills by jumping back and forth over her spider leg. Can she do this for the whole song?

> After making a spider, my sons decided to make other creatures with the materials, like a turtle and butterfly.
> —Lisa

Pumpkin Faces

Who needs jack-o'-lanterns when you can make paper pumpkin faces?

What You'll Need	All Ages	Baby	Toddler	Preschooler	School-Age Child
Child safe-scissors	🖑				
Orange and black construction paper	🖑				
Glue sticks	🖑				
Clear contact paper	🖑				

Help your children cut large ovals from orange construction paper—one oval for your baby and three for each of your other children. Also cut out triangles, circles, and squares from black construction paper—one set of shapes for your baby plus at least ten of each shape for each of your other children. Your children then can use the shapes as eyes, noses, mouths, and ears to turn the ovals into pumpkin faces, and you can create a face for your baby to explore.

Baby

Make a pumpkin face for your baby by gluing the shapes onto the oval, then cover it with clear contact paper. The contrast between orange and black will heighten her developing sense of color. Let her handle the pumpkin face while you point out its eyes, nose, and mouth, or ask her to point them out if she's old enough to identify facial features.

Toddler
Use this activity to review shapes with your toddler. Work alongside her as she decides which shapes to use for her pumpkin faces. She may want triangles or circles for eyes, for example. Dab glue on the pumpkin and let her press her shapes onto the glue.

Preschooler
Your preschooler understands the proper placement of facial features, but use this activity to encourage him to work abstractly. For example, he may use a circle for one eye and a square for the other. When his faces are complete, discuss the differences or similarities among them.

School-Age Child
Before your school-age child decorates his pumpkin faces, challenge him to turn the art project into a math project: Given the number of different shapes, how many combinations for eyes can he make (two circles, one circle and one square, two squares, and so on)? Encourage him to work out the problem by creating each combination of shapes on his pumpkin.

Spooky Chairs

These scary chair covers will create the perfect Halloween ambience for your kitchen or dining room.

What You'll Need	All Ages	Baby	Toddler	Preschooler	School-Age Child
Old pillowcases	✋				
White, black, or orange acrylic paint		✋			✋
Paintbrush		✋			✋
Wet wipes		✋			
Fabric marker		✋		✋	✋
Safety pins or masking tape		✋			
Halloween foam stickers (available at craft stores)			✋		✋
Cotton balls			✋		✋
Tacky glue			✋	✋	✋
Chalk				✋	✋
Black felt				✋	✋
Scissors				✋	✋

Encourage your children to have a ghoulishly good time decorating one side of their pillowcases. When they're done, slip each pillowcase over the back of a chair so the decorated side is facing out behind the chair.

Baby

Your baby can help design a pillowcase to decorate the back of her highchair. Cover the palm side of one of her hands with white paint, then gently press it onto a dark-colored pillowcase several times to make skeletal handprints. If you have only a light-colored pillowcase, paint your baby's palm (not her fingers) orange and press it onto the pillowcase to make pumpkins. Clean her hands with wet wipes when you're done. After the paint has dried, turn the pumpkins into jack-o'-lanterns by drawing features with a fabric marker. When it's complete, affix the pillowcase to the back of the highchair with safety pins (if the seat if cloth-covered) or masking tape (if the seat is plastic).

Toddler

Your toddler will enjoy decorating her pillowcase with Halloween-themed foam stickers, which may be easier for her to manipulate than regular stickers. She may need help peeling the backs off the stickers, but let her decide where to place them. With your help, she can also create ghosts using cotton balls and tacky glue. Simply pull the cotton balls apart so they are wispy.

Preschooler

Your preschooler can use chalk to draw spooky shapes on black felt, like a haunted house, witch hat, or bat. Cut out the shapes for him, and let him glue them onto his pillowcase. Have him write his name on his creation with a fabric marker.

School-Age Child

With felt, paint, cotton balls, stickers, chalk, and fabric markers, your school-age child will have lots of ways to decorate his pillowcase. Encourage him to use the entire pillowcase to create a graveyard scene or haunted house.

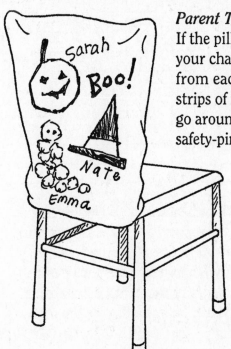

Parent Tip
If the pillowcases don't fit over your chairs, cut the decorated side from each pillowcase. Cut two strips of fabric just long enough to go around the back of a chair, then safety-pin one strip at the top of the decorated pillowcase piece and the other strip at the bottom to secure it to the chair.

Rock Pumpkins

Create a patch of rock pumpkins in your yard!

What You'll Need	All Ages	Baby	Toddler	Preschooler	School-Age Child
Baseball-size rocks	🖐				
Orange paint	🖐				
Zip-close plastic bag		🖐			
Black marker	🖐				
Disposable plastic container			🖐		
Paintbrush				🖐	🖐
Twigs					🖐
Green paint					🖐
Tacky glue					🖐

Take your children to a park or beach and collect several baseball-size rocks. (If necessary, purchase rocks from a craft store or landscaping center.) At home, rinse the rocks with warm water and let them dry. Then have your kids paint the rocks orange and use markers to turn them into jack-o'-lanterns. When finished, your children can help you display the rock pumpkins in your yard.

Baby

Your baby can "paint" rocks, too. Pour orange paint into a zip-close plastic bag and place three rocks inside it. Securely tape the bag closed. If your baby is six months or older, help him roll and shake the rocks inside the bag to coat the rocks with paint. If he is younger than six months, sit close to him so he can watch you roll and shake the bag. The bright-colored paint will catch his eye. Finish by adding jack-o'-lantern features with a marker.

Toddler

Given his increasing mastery of picking up items, your toddler will enjoy collecting rocks. To help him paint his rocks back home, pour paint into a disposable plastic container. He can carefully drop all of his rocks into the container and roll them around to paint them on all sides. When the paint is dry, have him tell you what expression you should draw on his pumpkins, or let him draw on them himself.

Preschooler

As you collect the rocks, encourage your preschooler to find ones that suit her fancy. Does she like bumpy or smooth ones? Tall or short ones? Skinny or fat ones? Her dexterity is becoming more controlled, so when she decorates the jack-o'-lanterns, challenge her to take her time with the paintbrush and markers.

School-Age Child

Your school-age child will put a lot of detail into painting her jack-o'-lanterns and drawing the features. As an added touch, she can paint little pieces of twigs green and then glue them as stems onto the tops of her jack-o'-lanterns. She may also want to glue stems onto her siblings' jack-o'-lanterns.

Thanks and Giving

During your Thanksgiving meal, serve a helping of love and appreciation with this simple sharing game.

What You'll Need	All Ages	Baby	Toddler	Preschooler	School-Age Child
Scarf (or other cloth item)	✋				

You can play this game anytime, but it's especially nice when extended family is seated for the Thanksgiving meal. To play, hand a scarf to one of your children and ask him to announce something for which he is thankful. Then have him compliment the person sitting to his left and give her the scarf. She then gives thanks and compliments the person on her left while passing on the scarf. The game ends when everyone has given thanks and compliments.

Baby

When it's your baby's turn to receive the scarf, let her hold it while you give thanks and compliment her neighbor on her behalf. For instance, you may say, "The baby is thankful for all the kisses she receives, and she loves how well her big sister reads books to her!" Tickle her with the scarf to entice a smile for her siblings and extended family.

Toddler

At this age, your toddler's world revolves mostly around his own wants and needs. This game will introduce to him gratitude and appreciation of others. Help him articulate his thankfulness by asking questions such as, "Are you thankful that it was sunny out today so you could play in the yard?" Use similar prompts to help him compliment his neighbor.

Preschooler

Your preschooler may express thanks for seemingly trivial items like toys or books, but they bring him joy. Resist leading his responses. Receiving compliments may be your preschooler's favorite part of the game. He is becoming aware of other people's feelings of him and will love hearing that he is an important member of the family.

School-Age Child

In this sharing time, ask your school-age child to share something positive and appreciative about all her siblings, rather than just the person on her left. This exercise will hopefully strengthen the sibling bonds. For example, she might say she enjoys having the baby as the newest member of the family, she loves the toddler's energy, and she admires how the preschooler has learned to write his name.

Parent Tip
Don't forget you get a turn, too. Make sure you compliment each of your children. They need to hear your praise!

Handprint Menorahs

Your children can use their handprints to create a menorah, one of the oldest symbols of the Jewish faith.

What You'll Need	All Ages	Baby	Toddler	Preschooler	School-Age Child
Construction paper	✋				
Paintbrushes	✋				
Washable tempera paint	✋				
Wet wipes	✋				
Crayons				✋	✋
Child-safe scissors				✋	✋
Glue sticks				✋	✋

Give each child a sheet of construction paper. Use a paintbrush to lightly paint the palm side of their hands. Have them press one hand onto the paper then press the other hand next to it so the thumbs overlap. The eight fingers represent candles, which in turn represent the eight nights of Hanukkah. The overlapping thumbprints represent the shamash, the special candle used to light the others. When they are done, clean their hands with wet wipes.

Baby

After you've made a menorah with your baby's hands, let her enjoy making additional handprints on another sheet of paper with the paint remaining on her hands. She may likely slap and bang her hands to make a delightfully loud noise. See if she'll slap her hands in response after you slap down your hands. Just be sure she doesn't put her hands in her mouth.

Toddler
Your toddler is learning about numbers and counting. As you make her menorah, count the candles together forward and backward.

Preschooler and School-Age Child
To prepare for "lighting" the candles in the nights ahead, your preschooler and school-age child can team up to draw and cut out small "flames" from yellow construction paper. They will need nine flames for each sibling's menorah. When they're done, have them glue a flame to each shamash. Then on each night of Hanukkah, they can glue a flame to another candle on each menorah.

Parent Tip
Teach your children the history of Hanukkah and the menorah. Here are some great books to read together: *It's Hanukkah!* by Santiago Cohen, *Festival of Lights: The Story of Hanukkah* by Maida Silverman, and *Hanukkah, Oh Hanukkah!* by Susan L. Roth.

Dreidel Animals

Your family will act like animals with this "spin" on a traditional Jewish game!

What You'll Need	All Ages	Baby	Toddler	Preschooler	School-Age Child
Paper and pencil	🖐				
Dreidel (or see page 420 to make one)	🖐				

Have your children come up with as many animals that begin with the letters *G, H,* and *S* as they can. Jot down their answers on a sheet of paper. Here are some ideas:

- *G*: Giraffe, grasshopper, gazelle, goat, goose
- *H*: Horse, hummingbird, hawk, hippopotamus
- *S*: Snake, sheep, seal, spider, swan

Next, sit in a circle around a hard surface and take turns spinning a dreidel. Tell your children that when the dreidel stops face-up on *G, H,* or *S,* the person who spun it must move and sound like an animal that begins with that letter. For example, if the *G* is face-up, the spinner can honk and waddle like a goose. Use your list of animals to provide ideas, if necessary. To make the game more challenging, when the *N* is face-up, the spinner may move and sound like any animal he chooses. After the spinner has acted like an animal for at least ten seconds, the others may try to identify the animal, then copy the movements and sounds!

Baby

Spin the dreidel for your baby and help him move like the appropriate animal. For instance, if the *H* lands face-up and you choose a horse, hold him face-out against your chest (supporting his head and neck) while you gallop around. He'll love the action! If you like, make the appropriate animal sounds for your baby as well.

Toddler

When it's your toddler's turn, help him spin the dreidel. Or have him hold the dreidel with both hands, shake it, then drop it to reveal a letter. Help him identify the face-up letter, whisper the names of two animals that begin with that letter, then let him choose one to act out.

Preschooler and School-Age Child

As a challenge, ask your preschooler and school-age child to give the other players hints rather than act like animals during a few of their turns. For instance, your preschooler may say, "This animal likes to eat hay" (horse). Your school-age may say, "The animal I am thinking of can fly backward" (hummingbird).

Homemade Dreidel
Single-serving milk or juice carton
Tape
Plain paper
Pen or marker
Scissors
¼-inch dowel or unsharpened pencil

Flatten the top of the carton and tape it down securely. Cover the carton with plain paper. On each side, write one of the letters *N*, *G*, *H*, and *S* to represent the first letters in the four words of the Hebrew message *nes gadol hayah sham*, which means "A great miracle happened there." (Hebrew characters are read from right to left.)

Poke a small hole in the centers of the top and bottom of the carton and push the dowel or pencil through both holes to make a spinning top.

These directions are adapted from *The Arts and Crafts Busy Book* by Trish Kuffner (Meadowbrook Press).

Merry Mini-Houses

These tiny, tasty houses are sure to get your kids in the holiday mood!

What You'll Need	All Ages	Baby	Toddler	Preschooler	School-Age Child
Wax paper			🖐	🖐	🖐
Paintbrushes and small bowls			🖐	🖐	🖐
Ready-made frosting			🖐	🖐	🖐
Graham crackers	🖐				
Edible decorations, including cereal, fruit snacks, diced fruit, and so on		🖐			
Yogurt		🖐			

Lay wax paper in front of your toddler, preschooler, and school-age child to use as a workspace. Give them each a paintbrush and a small bowl of frosting. Show your kids how to use the frosting to glue together four graham cracker halves to make the walls of a house. Add two graham cracker halves at a slant to create a roof for the house. Finally, have them decorate the houses by attaching cereal, fruit snacks, diced fruit, and other edible items with the frosting. Let the frosting harden before displaying (or eating!) the mini-houses.

Baby

As your baby's siblings build their mini-houses, make a mini-creation he can enjoy: Spread some yogurt on a graham cracker and decorate it with diced fruit. As he watches his siblings build with the graham crackers, he'll try to do the same. If he's not eating solids yet, supervise closely if he tries to put the items in his mouth. Chances are, he'll be too busy playing to eat!

Toddler

Although you will likely build your toddler's mini-house, she can decorate it. Show her how to gently paint frosting onto the house and stick decorations onto it. A house with a flat roof may make an easier surface for her to decorate.

Preschooler and School-Age Child

Encourage your preschooler and school-age child to decorate their mini-houses in detail. For example, they can create the outlines of doors or window frames with the small cereal pieces. They can make walkways, chimneys, and more!

Rudolph Says

Gather your kids for this game of Simon Says with a
Christmas twist.

What You'll Need	All Ages	Baby	Toddler	Preschooler	School-Age Child
Red construction paper	🖐				
Scissors	🖐				
Tape	🖐				

In a room with a lot of open space, tell your kids how to play
this game: Instead of Simon Says, it's Rudolph the Red-Nosed
Reindeer Says. Rudolph will make a command, such as "put
your hand on your head," "jump up and down," "turn around
in a circle," and so on. Everyone else must follow the command,
but only if Rudolph prefaces it with "Rudolph says…" If Rudolph
doesn't say this preface, everyone else must stay still. Choose a
child to be Rudolph first and affix a small red circle of construction paper to his nose with tape. Play the game until each child
has had a chance to be Rudolph.

Baby and Toddler

With your help, your baby and toddler can follow the commands.
Your toddler will probably do the action regardless of whether
Rudolph prefaces the command with "Rudolph says…" That's
okay. At this age, he may not understand the nuance of the

game, but it's still good for him to practice following an explicit command!

When it's their turn to be Rudolph, the red circle on the nose will fascinate your little ones. Be sure to let them see themselves as Rudolph in a mirror. While you'll have to give commands for your baby Rudolph, your toddler Rudolph will likely love to tell his siblings what to do. Prompt your older kids to do the action even if your toddler doesn't preface his command with "Rudolph says…"

Preschooler and School-Age Child

This game is a great way for your preschooler and school-age child to practice their listening skills. See how well they can follow the rules. When it's their turns to be Rudolph, encourage them to give commands that reflect Christmas or winter activities. For example, "pretend to wrap gifts" or "sing 'Rudolph the Red-Nosed Reindeer.'"

Did You Know?
The tale of "Rudolph the Red-Nosed Reindeer" was first told in 1939. Ever since, children around the world have looked for his red nose leading Santa's sleigh in the dark sky on Christmas Eve.

A Handful of Christmas

Spread the holiday cheer with this handprint Christmas tree.

What You'll Need	All Ages	Baby	Toddler	Preschooler	School-Age Child
Green construction paper	🖐				
Pencils	🖐				
Child-safe scissors	🖐				
Large sheet of white paper	🖐				
Star stickers			🖐	🖐	🖐
Glue and tinsel			🖐	🖐	🖐

Help your children trace their hands on green construction paper and cut out the tracings. To complete the tree, you'll need twenty-one hand cutouts, so enlist your older children's help with this step! Show your older children how to glue the cutouts (fingers pointing up) onto a large sheet of white paper in six rows of descending number. That is, they will glue a row of six hands along the bottom, then a row of five hands above and slightly overlapping the row of six, then a row of four hands slightly overlapping the row of five, and so on.

Baby

As you trace your baby's hand, entertain her with the following action poem:

This little elf's family is as happy as can be, be, be.
  (Trace the thumb.)
They are all full of glee, glee, glee.
  (Trace the index finger.)
"Yes," the family cheered, "We, we, we
  (Trace the middle finger.)
have been waiting since you were born, born, born
  (Trace the ring finger.)
to say, 'Wake up! It's Christmas morn, morn, morn!'"
  (Trace the pinky.)

Toddler, Preschooler, and School-Age Child

When the tree is complete, they can decorate it with star stickers and also glue on some tinsel. To create special ornaments, have them each cut out a circle from colored construction paper. You or your school-age child can then write their favorite things about Christmas on their ornaments before gluing them onto the tree.

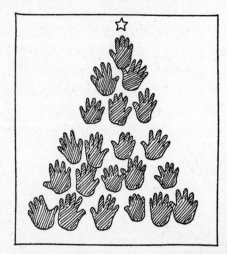

Parent Tip
Remember to date the tree. It's a great keepsake to display year after year.

Past and Future

Kwanzaa is a holiday to remind African Americans of their important past and promising future. Here's a fun game that will have your children happily moving backward and forward.

What You'll Need	All Ages	Baby	Toddler	Preschooler	School-Age Child
Plastic cups	👋				
Pencils	👋				
Red, black, and green construction paper	👋				
Child-safe scissors	👋				
Silver marker	👋				
Basket	👋				

Help your children use plastic cups to trace circles on the construction paper. Trace and cut out four circles on red paper, two on black, and two on green (the colors of Kwanzaa). With a marker, you or your school-age child can write the number 1 on the red circles, the number 2 on the black circles, and the number 3 on the green circles. Write the word *forward* on two red circles, one black circle, and one green circle. Then write the word *backward* on the remaining circles. Place all the circles in a basket.

Next, designate a starting point and a finishing point in your play area. Have your kids stand at the starting point and take turns drawing a circle from the basket with eyes closed.

The child then reads the card to determine how many steps he may take forward or backward. The game ends when a child reaches the finishing point.

Baby
Your baby can play this game, too, with your help. If she can grasp objects, let her draw a circle from the basket when it's her turn. If she's showing signs of standing or walking, help her step forward or backward as her card dictates. Even if she's just in your arms, she'll enjoy the movement and being close to you and her siblings.

Toddler
This game is a great opportunity to teach your toddler about colors and numbers. When he draws a circle, ask him to first identify its color. Then help him identify the number of steps to take and in what direction. Be sure to count with him.

Preschooler and School-Age Child
To emphasize the idea of the past and future, encourage your older children to make a wish for the future when they move forward and remember a proud moment from the past when they move backward. For example, when your preschooler draws a circle that has her move forward, she may say, "I wish to learn to ride my bike in the future." When your school-age child draws a circle that has him move backward, he may say, "I'm proud I've learned to ice-skate."

Index

A

ABC Games, 176
Act It Out, 90
Adopt a Family Tree, 265
All About Us, 194
Animal Hospital, 58
Apple Art, 315
Apple Taste Test, 397
Aquapella, 97
At the End of a Rainbow, 365
At the Movies, 41

B

Backyard Parade, The, 132
Ball In, Out, and About, 122
Bark Rubbings, 187
Barnyard Fun, 52
Beanbag Race, 160
Birdbath Haven, A, 260
Bounce to the Beat, 107
Build It Up!, 15

C

Camping In, 50
Canvas Painting, 309
Charity Roundup, 269
Checkup at the Doctor's Office, 56
Check-Us-Out Library, 44
Child's Touch Bracelet, A, 379
Cinco de Mayo Piñatas, 377
Clap! Snap! Stomp!, 113
Collection Binders, 22
Colorful Collages, 302
Columbus Day Sailing Hats, 401
Cool School Days, 67
Crazy Sheet, 13

D

Dancing with Feeling, 105
Day in the Life of Daddy, 388
Designer Dress Up, 39
Diddle, Diddle, Doo, 172
Dining Out, 69
Doing the Bubble Pop, 371
Dreidel Animals, 418

F

Faces Fit for a Frame, 323
Family Letter, 239
Fashion from around the World, 272
Feather Frenzy, 17
Feed All the Little Birds, 258
Feel-Good New Year's Fortunes, 358
Five-Minute Scrambled Eggs, 338
Food Pyramids, 206
Fragrant Cinnamon Buns, 347
Freeze!, 166
Fruity Pastry Cups, 343
Fruity Tie-Dye Shirts, 299

G

Get-Well Basket, 253
Give Me an A!, 84
Goobly-Goop, 307
Grandparents Day Video, 395
Great Easter Egg Search, The, 375
Green, Yellow, Red Lights, 134
Groundhog Day Silhouettes, 360

H

Handful of Christmas, A, 425
Handprint Menorahs, 416
Having a Rolling Ball, 2

Head, Shoulders, Knees,
   and Toes, 215
Hello and Goodbye!, 256
Helping Hands, 236
Hide-and-Seek Sounds, 4
Hokey-Pokey Family, 115
Home Highway, The, 27
Homemade Applesauce, 351
Homemade Butter, 349
Hoop Ball Toss, 9
Hop with Me, 162
Hungry Wolf, 130

I

Icy Shapes, 295
If the Shoe Fits, 65
Indoor Scavenger Hunt, 29
Invisible Baseball, 109
It's a Jungle Out There, 78
It's a Wrap, 25

J

Jazzin' Up Junk Mail, 11

K

King and Queen Crowns, 304

L

Leaf Place Mats, 399
Leprechaun Race, 368
Let Me See Your Funny Face, 276
Let Our Feet Do the Painting, 330
Let's All Pitch In, 251
Let's Go Grocery Shopping, 72
Let's Go to the Library, 218
Letterboxing, 146
Little Gymnasts, 103
Look at Us Now Murals, 282

M

Mac & Cheese, 339
Mail for You and Me, 46
Make a Rainbow, 211
Marvelous Marble Roll, 297
Me and My Family Scrapbook, 226
Merry Mini-Houses, 421
Money! Money! Money!, 220
Morning Stretches, 76
Mother's Day Window Box, 381
Moving around the World, 263
Muddy Day at the Farm, 293

N

Name Plates, 213
New Musical Chairs, 99
Number Match Up, 200

O

Oatmeal Pancakes, 344
Opposite Olympics, 192
Our Family Tree, 228
Our Own Terrariums, 153

P

Packin' a Picnic, 19
Past and Future, 427
Patriotic Wreath, 384
Paws and Claws, 138
Phone Book Fun, 209
Pick a Move, 82
Pineapple Pops, 355
Pipe Cleaner Flowers, 317
Pizza Faces, 342
Planes, Trains, and Automobiles, 60
Pop Stars, 101
Pop! Go Our Bodies, 86
Portable Seas, 284
Pumpkin Faces, 407
Puzzle Making, 35

Q

Questions in the Jar, 231

R

Raking 'Em Up, 149
Recyclables, 327
Recycling Center, 267
Ring Those Bells, 116
Rock Pumpkins, 412
Royal Birthday Throne, A, 245
Rudolph Says, 423

S

S'mores Creatures, 352
Sand Discoveries, 124
Seashell Magnets, 393
Shadow, Shadow on the Wall, 6
Shake It, 80
Shapely Mural, A, 222
Sharing a Smile, 33
Show Me a Sign, 242
Show-and-Tell Me, 249
Signs of Spring, 373
Soaring with Scarves, 92
Spider Games, 404
Spin the Storybox, 184

Spin, Spin Pinwheel, 320
Splendid Smoothies, 354
Spooky Chairs, 409
Sprinkler Race, 151
Squeeze Me Sponge Art, 280
Stargazing, 128
Start Your Day Right, 233
Stay Still Art, 311
Sticking to Our ABCs, 190
Strollin' through Nature, 120
Summer Solstice Sun Catchers, 390
Sunflower, Shine for Me, 136
Surprise Designs, 313
Sweet-and-Salty Snack, 353

T

Table Memory, 168
Taco Volcano, 341
Tasty Banana Bread, 345
Ten Things, 178
Terrific Tunnels, 37
Thanks and Giving, 414
These Little Kids Went to the
    Market, 170
Time Capsule, 247
Toasted Banana Treat, 346

Toy Store Sale, 48

Trace a Place Mat, 278

Twig-and-Rock Houses, 155

U

Up, Up, Paper Airplane, 157

Uppity-Do Hairdressers, 54

V

Very Cool Fruity Play Dough, 332

Village to Call Our Own, A, 290

W

Walk in My Steps, 111

Walk on the Moon, 63

Watching the Clouds Pass By, 144

Water "Painting", 142

Wave That Flag, 386

We've Got the Beat, 88

Weather Watch, 197

Welcome to Water World, 126

What Do You Hear?, 180

What Floats?, 204

Where Is Everyone Going?, 174

Where Is the Boat?, 31

Wild Animal Flashcards, 325

Wild Wheel of Color, 287

Window Painting, 202

Won't Knock Us Down, 140

Y

Yoga, 94

You're in My Heart, 362